DEATH:
THE GREAT ADVENTURE

DEATH:
THE GREAT
ADVENTURE

COMPILED BY TWO STUDENTS

From the Writings of
Alice A. Bailey
and
The Tibetan Master, Djwhal Khul

LUCIS PUBLISHING COMPANY
New York

LUCIS PRESS, LTD.
London

This compilation is extracted from books by Alice A. Bailey for which the Lucis Trust holds copyrights.

ISBN No. 0-85330-138-7

First Printing, 1985
Third Printing, 1998

The Lucis Publishing Company is a non-profit organisation owned by the Lucis Trust. No royalties are paid on this book.

This title has been translated into Danish, Dutch, French, German, and Spanish. Translation into other languages is proceeding.

LUCIS PUBLISHING COMPANY
120 Wall Street
New York, NY 10005

LUCIS PRESS, LTD.
Suite 54
3 Whitehall Court
London SW1A 2EF

MANUFACTURED IN THE UNITED STATES OF AMERICA
By Fort Orange Press, Inc., Albany, NY

EXTRACT FROM A STATEMENT
BY THE TIBETAN

Suffice it to say, that I am a Tibetan disciple of a certain degree, and this tells you but little, for all are disciples from the humblest aspirant up to, and beyond, the Christ Himself. I live in a physical body like other men, on the borders of Tibet, and at times (from the exoteric standpoint) preside over a large group of Tibetan lamas, when my other duties permit. It is this fact that has caused it to be reported that I am an abbot of this particular lamasery. Those associated with me in the work of the Hierarchy (and all true disciples are associated in this work) know me by still another name and office. A.A.B. knows who I am and recognises me by two of my names.

I am a brother of yours, who has travelled a little longer upon the Path than has the average student, and has therefore incurred greater responsibilities. I am one who has wrestled and fought his way into a greater measure of light than has the aspirant who will read this article, and I must therefore act as a transmitter of the light, no matter what the cost. I am not an old man, as age counts among the teachers, yet I am not young or inexperienced. My work is to teach and spread the knowledge of the Ageless Wisdom wherever I can find a response, and I have been doing this for many years. I seek also to help the Master M. and the Master K. H. whenever opportunity offers, for I have been long connected with Them and with Their work. In all the above, I have told you much; yet at the same time I have told you nothing which would lead you to offer me that blind obedience and the foolish devotion which the emotional aspirant offers to the Guru and Master Whom he is as yet unable to contact. Nor will he make that desired contact until he has transmuted emotional devotion into unselfish service to humanity — not to the Master.

The books that I have written are sent out with no claim for their acceptance. They may, or may not, be correct, true and useful. It is for you to ascertain their truth by right practice and by the exercise of the intuition. Neither I or A. A. B. is the least interested in having them acclaimed as inspired writings, or in having anyone speak of them (with bated breath) as being the work of one of the Masters. If they present truth in such a way that it follows sequentially upon that already offered in the world teachings, if the information given raises the aspiration and the will-to-serve from the plane of the emotions to that of the mind (the plane whereon the Masters *can* be found), then they will have served their purpose. If the teaching conveyed calls forth a response from the illumined mind of the worker in the world, and brings a flashing forth of his intuition, then let that teaching be accepted. But not otherwise. If the statements meet with eventual corroboration, or are deemed true under the test of the Law of Correspondences, then that is well and good. But should this not be so, let not the student accept what is said.

August 1934

REFERENCE INDEX

BOOKS BY THE TIBETAN (DJWHAL KHUL)
through ALICE A. BAILEY

NOTE

Reference Example: A reference number, such as for instance (12-135/6) at the end of a quotation, would refer to a quotation taken from *"Education in the New Age"* (12) starting on page 135, and continued on page 136.

THE GREAT INVOCATION

From the point of Light within the Mind of God
  Let light stream forth into the minds of men.
    Let Light descend on Earth.

From the point of Love within the Heart of God
  Let love stream forth into the hearts of men.
    May Christ return to Earth.

From the centre where the Will of God is known
  Let purpose guide the little wills of men—
    The purpose which the Masters know and serve.

From the centre which we call the race of men
  Let the Plan of Love and Light work out
    And may it seal the door where evil dwells.

Let Light and Love and Power restore the Plan on Earth.

    The above Invocation or Prayer does not belong to any person or group, but to all Humanity. The beauty and the strength of this Invocation lies in its simplicity, and in its expression of certain central truths which all men, innately and normally, accept— the truth of the existence of a basic Intelligence to Whom we vaguely give the name of God; the truth that behind all outer seeming, the motivating power of the universe is Love; the truth that a great Individuality came to earth, called by Christians, the Christ, and embodied that love so that we could understand; the truth that both love and intelligence are effects of what is called the Will of God; and finally the self-evident truth that only through *humanity* itself can the Divine Plan work out.

Alice A. Bailey

TABLE OF CONTENTS

"Bear in mind, O Chela, that within the known spheres naught is but light responsive to the WORD. Know that that light descends and concentrates itself; know that from its point of chosen focus, it lightens its own sphere; know too that light ascends and leaves in darkness that which it—in time and space—illuminated. This descending and ascension men call life, existence and decease; this We Who tread the Lighted Way call death, experience and life.

ESOTERIC HEALING, (VOLUME IV)
(A TREATISE ON THE SEVEN RAYS)
p. 468

PROLOGUE

I. This, our present cycle, is the end of the age, and the next two hundred years will see the abolition of death, as we now understand that great transition, and the establishing of the fact of the soul's existence.   (14-96)

II. Our ideas about death have been erroneous; we have looked upon it as the great and ultimate terror, whereas in reality it is the great escape, the entrance into a fuller measure of activity, and the release of the life from the crystallised vehicle and an inadequate form.   (19-64/5)

III. Why not welcome Transition? Learn to glory in experience, which is the gift of wise old age, and look forward to the Great Adventure which confronts you. You know well — in your highest moments — that Transition means realisation without any physical plane limitations.   (6-696)

IV. Disease and death are essentially conditions inherent in substance; just as long as man identifies himself with the form aspect, so will he be conditioned by the Law of Dissolution. This law is a fundamental and natural law governing the life of the form in all the kingdoms of nature.   (17-501)

V. There is a technique of dying just as there is of living . . . .   (4-302)

VI. . . . [People] fail to relate death and sleep. Death, after all, is only a longer interval in the life of physical plane functioning; one has only "gone abroad" for a longer period.   (4-495)

VII. . . . death can be best regarded as the experience which frees us from the illusion of form . . . .   (22-243)

VIII. . . . death is only an interlude in a life of steadily accumulating experience . . . it marks a definite transition from one <u>state of consciousness into another</u>.   (22-242)

IX. *Death comes to the individual man, in the ordinary sense of the term, when the will-to-live in a physical body goes and the will-to-abstract takes its place. This we call death. (18-164/5)*

X. *As humanity becomes soul-conscious ... death will be seen as an "ordered" process, carried out in full consciousness and with understanding of cyclic purpose.   (17-435/6)*

XI. *... The Work of Restitution ... The Art of Elimination ... The Processes of Integration ... These three processes are death.   (17-394/5)*

XII. *Death is an act of the intuition, transmitted by the soul to the personality and then acted upon in conformity to the divine will by the individual will.   (16-599)*

XIII. *And then a Word sounds forth. The descended, radiating point of light ascends, responsive to the dimly heard recalling note, attracted to its emanating source. This man calls death and this the soul calls life.   (17-469)*

XIV. *Resurrection is the keynote of nature; death is not. Death is only the ante-chamber of resurrection.   (13-469)*

PART I

This, our present cycle, is the end of the age, and the next two hundred years will see the abolition of death, as we now understand that great transition, and the establishing of the fact of the soul's existence.   (14-96)

PART I

(1)   THE SOUL will be known as an entity, as the motivating impulse and the spiritual centre back of all manifested forms. The next few decades will see certain great beliefs substantiated. The work of Christ, and His main mission two thousand years ago, was to demonstrate the divine possibilities and powers latent in every human being. The proclamation which He made to the effect that we were all sons of God and own one universal Father will, in the future, no longer be regarded as a beautiful, mystical and symbolic statement, but will be regarded as a scientific pronouncement. Our universal brotherhood and our essential immortality will be demonstrated and realised to be facts in nature.   (14-96)

(2)   It takes courage to face the fact of death, and to formulate with definiteness one's beliefs upon the subject. . . .

     Death is the only event which we can predict with absolute certainty, and yet it is the event about which the majority of human beings refuse to think at all until faced with the imminent and personal issue. People face death in many different ways; some bring to the adventure a feeling of self-pity, and are so occupied with what they have to leave behind, what is about to end for them, and the relinquishing of all they have gathered in life, that the true significance of the inevitable future fails to arrest their attention. Others face it with courage, making the best of what may not be evaded, and look up into the face of death with a gallant gesture because there is nothing else they can do. Their pride helps them to encounter the event. Still others refuse altogether to consider the possibility; they hypnotise themselves into a condition wherein the thought of death is refused all lodgement in their consciousness, and they will not consider its possibility, so that when it comes, it catches them unawares; they are left helpless and unable to do more than simply die. The Christian attitude, as a rule, is more definitely an acceptance of the will of God, with the resolution to regard the happening as therefore the best of happenings, even if it does not seem so from the angle of environment and circumstance. A steadfast belief in God and His predestined purpose for the individual carries them triumphantly through the gate of death, but if one told them that this was simply another form of the fatalism of the Eastern thinker, and a fixed belief in an unalterable destiny, they would regard it as untrue. They hide behind the name of God.

Death can, however, be more than these things, and can be met in a different way. It can be made to hold a definite place in life and thought, and we can prepare for it as something which cannot be evaded, but which is simply the Bringer of Changes. Thus we make the process of death a planned part of our entire life purpose. We can *live* with the consciousness of immortality, and it will give an added colouring and beauty to life; we can foster the awareness of our future transition, and live with the expectation of its wonder. Death thus faced, and regarded as a prelude to further living experience, takes on a different meaning. It becomes a mystical experience, a form of initiation, finding its culminating point in the Crucifixion. All previous lesser renunciations prepare us for the great renunciation; all earlier deaths are but the prelude for the stupendous episode of dying. Death brings us release—temporary perhaps, though eventually permanent—from the body nature, from existence on the physical plane and its visible experience. It is a setting free from limitation; and whether one believes (as many millions do) that death is only an interlude in a life of steadily accumulating experience, or the end of all such experience (as many other millions hold), there is no denying the fact that it marks a definite transition from one *state of consciousness into another.*   (22-240/2)

(3)   Religious students will study the side of manifestation we call the "life side" just as the scientist studies that called "matter," and both will come to a realisation of the close relation existing between the two, and thus the old gap and the ancient warfare between science and religion will be in temporary abeyance. Definite methods of demonstrating the fact that life persists after the death of the physical body will be followed, and the etheric web will be recognised as a factor in the case.   (3-429)

(4)   The first step towards substantiating the fact of the soul is to establish the fact of survival though this may not necessarily

prove the fact of immortality. It can nevertheless be regarded as a step in the right direction. That something survives the process of death, and that something persists after the disintegration of the physical body, is steadily being proved. If that is not so, then we are the victims of a collective hallucination, and the brains and minds of thousands of people are untrue and deceiving, are diseased and distorted. Such a gigantic collective insanity is more difficult to credit than the alternative of an expanded consciousness. This development along psychic lines does not prove the fact of the soul, however; it only serves to break down the materialistic position.   (14-98/9)

(5)   The problem of death, needless to say, is founded upon the love of life which is the deepest instinct in human nature. The determination that nothing is lost under divine law is a recognition of science; eternal persistence in some form or another is universally held to be a truth. Out of the welter of theories, three major solutions have been proposed; these are well known to all thinking people. They are:

1. *The strictly materialistic solution,* which posits the experience and expression of conscious life as long as the physical, tangible form exists and persists, but also teaches that after death and the subsequent disintegration of the body there is no longer any conscious, functioning, self-identified person. The sense of the "I," the awareness of a personality in contradistinction to all other personalities, vanishes with the disappearance of the form; personality is believed to be only the sumtotal of the consciousness of the cells in the body. This theory relegates man to the same state as any of the other forms in the three other kingdoms in nature; it is based on the nonsensitivity of the average human being to life, withdrawn from a tangible vehicle; it ignores all evidence to the contrary and says that because we cannot see (visually) and prove (tangibly) the persistence of the "I" or the immortal entity after death, it is nonexistent. This theory is not held by so many as it was in earlier years, particularly during the materialistic Victorian age.
2. *The theory of conditional immortality.* This theory is still held by certain fundamentalist and theologically narrow schools of thought and also by a few of the intelligentsia, primarily those of egoistic tendency. It posits that only those who reach a particular stage of spiritual awareness, or who accept a peculiar set of

theological pronouncements, can receive the gift of personal immortality. The highly intellectual also argue at times that the crowning gift to humanity is a developed and cultured mind, and that those who possess this gift are likewise endowed with eternal persistence. One school dismisses those who are what they regard as spiritually recalcitrant or negative to the imposition of their particular theological certainties, either to complete annihilation as in the materialistic solution, or to a process of eternal punishment, thus at the same time arguing for a form of immortality.

Owing to the innate kindness of the human heart, very few are vindictive or unthinking enough to regard this presentation as acceptable, and of course among those we must class the unthinking people who escape from mental responsibility into a blind belief in theological pronouncements. The Christian interpretation as given by the orthodox and the fundamentalist schools proves untenable when submitted to clear reasoning; among the arguments which negate its accuracy lies the fact that Christianity posits a long future but no past; it is likewise a future entirely dependent upon the activities of this present life episode and accounts in no way for the distinctions and differences which distinguish humanity. It is only tenable upon the theory of an anthropomorphic Deity Whose will—as it works out in practice—gives a present that has no past but only a future; the injustice of this is widely recognised, but the inscrutable will of God must not be questioned. Millions still hold this belief, but it is not so strongly held as it was one hundred years ago.

3. *The theory of reincarnation,* so familiar to all my readers, is becoming increasingly popular in the Occident; it has always been accepted (though with many foolish additions and interpretations) in the Orient. This teaching has been as much distorted as have the teachings of the Christ or the Buddha or Shri Krishna by their narrow-minded and mentally limited theologians. The basic facts of a spiritual origin, of a descent into matter, of an ascent through the medium of constant incarnations in form until those forms are perfect expressions of the indwelling spiritual consciousness, and of a series of initiations at the close of the cycle of incarnation, are being more readily accepted and acknowledged than ever before.

Such are the major solutions of the problems of immortality and of the persistence of the human soul; they aim to answer the eternal questioning of the human heart as to Whence, Why, Whither and Where?   (17-400/2)

(6)   Within the next few years the fact of persistence and of the eternity of existence will have advanced out of the realm of questioning into the realm of certainty. . . . There will be no question in anyone's mind that the discarding of the physical body will leave a man still a conscious living entity. He will be known to be perpetuating his existence in a realm lying behind the physical. He will be known to be still alive, awake and aware. This will be brought about by:

a. The development of a power within the physical eye of a human being . . . will reveal the etheric body . . . men will be seen occupying that body.
b. The growth of the number of people who have the power to use the "reawakened third eye" will demonstrate immortality, for they will with facility see the man who has discarded his etheric body as well as his physical body.
c. A discovery in the field of photography will prove survival.
d. Through the use of the radio by those who have passed over will communication eventually be set up and reduced to a true science.
e. Man will eventually be keyed up to a perception and to a contact which will enable him to *see through,* which will reveal the nature of the fourth dimension, and will blend the subjective and objective worlds together into a new world. Death will lose its terrors and that particular fear will come to an end.   (17)-412/3)

(7)   It will be obvious to you that when humanity attains this outlook upon the fact of death or the art of dying, the entire attitude of the race of men will undergo beneficent change. This will be paralleled, as time elapses, by a rapport between men upon telepathic levels; men will be steadily growing in intelligence, and humanity will be increasingly focussed upon mental levels. This telepathic rapport will be a common and ordinary phenomenon of which modern spiritualism is the guarantee, though the distortion (and a very serious distortion) is largely based on humanity's wishful thinking, with very little true telepathy to be found in it. The

telepathy which *is* present today between the medium (in or out of trance) and the bereaved relative or friend is *not* between the one who has experienced the release of death and the one who is still in form. This should be remembered. In the interim where mind is not normally telepathic, there may be (though there very seldom is) the interposition of a mediumship based upon clairvoyance and clairaudience, but *not* upon trance. This will still necessitate a contact via a third party, and will be entirely astral; it will therefore be full of glamour and error. It will, however, be a step forward from the present mediumistic performances which simply ignore the man who is dead and give to the enquirer only what the medium reads in his aura—his recollection of the personal appearance, significant remembrances stored in the enquirer's consciousness, and wishful thinking anent advice demanded because the enquirer believes that because a man is dead he must be more wise than heretofore. When the medium at times succeeds in establishing true communication, it is because the enquirer and the dead person are mental types, and there is therefore a true telepathic rapport between them which the medium intercepts.

The race is progressing, developing and becoming increasingly mental. The relation between the dead and the living must and will be upon mental levels, prior to the processes of integration; the true severance of communication will come when the human soul is reabsorbed into the oversoul, prior to again reincarnating. The fact of communication up to that time will, however, completely destroy the fear of death. In the case of disciples working in a Master's Ashram, even this process of integration will constitute no barrier.   (17-395/6)

(8)   Thus we shall gradually find emerging in the world a large body of trained psychics whose powers are understood and who function on the astral plane with as much intelligence as they function on the physical plane, and who are preparing themselves for the expression of the higher psychic powers—spiritual perception and telepathy. These people will constitute eventually a body of linking souls, mediating between those who cannot see and hear on the astral plane because they are the prisoners of the physical body and those who are equally the prisoners of the astral plane, lacking the physical response apparatus.

The great need, therefore, is not that we should cease to consult and train our psychics and mediums, but that we should train them rightly and guard them intelligently and so link, through their means, the two worlds of the physical and the astral.   (13-15)

(9)   As time progresses and before the close of the next century, death will be finally seen to be non-existent in the sense in which it is now understood. Continuity of consciousness will be so widely developed and so many of the highest types of men will function simultaneously in the two worlds that the old fear will go and the intercourse between the astral plane and the physical plane will be so firmly established and so scientifically controlled that the work of the trance mediums will rightly and mercifully come to an end.   (4-301)

(10)   I would like to point out also that trance mediumship, as it is called, must inevitably be superseded by that mediumship which is offered by the man or woman who is clairvoyant or clair-audient on the astral plane, and who therefore in full waking consciousness and with the physical brain alert and active can offer himself as an intermediary between men in physical plane bodies (and therefore blind and deaf on the subtler levels) and those who, having discarded their bodies, are cut off from physical communication. This type of psychic can communicate with both groups and their value and their usefulness as mediums is beyond computation when they are singleminded, unselfish, pure and dedicated to service. But in the training to which they subject themselves they must avoid the present negative methods, and instead of "sitting for development" in a blank and waiting silence, they should endeavour to work positively as souls, remaining in conscious and intelligent possession of the lower mechanism of their bodies; they must know which centre in that body they use whilst working psychically, and they must learn to look out, *as souls,* upon the world of illusion in which they are undertaking to work; from their high and pure position let them see clearly, hear truly and report accurately, and so serve their age and generation, and make the astral plane a familiar and well-known place of activity, accustoming mankind to a state of existence wherein are found their fellowmen, experiencing, living and following the Path.   (13-12/3)

(11)   In the coming Aquarian Age we shall see humanity producing a culture which is sensitive to the finer and higher

spiritual values, a civilisation which is free from glamour and from much of the illusion which today colours the Aryan peoples, and a racial life which will be embodied in those forms which will bridge the gap at present existing; it will be free from what we now know as disease of the worst kind, though death and certain forms of bodily breakdown which may eventually end in death will, of course, still be prevalent. The overcoming of death is not contingent upon the elimination of bodily ills, but upon the establishing of that continuity of consciousness which carries over from the physical plane of life to the inner subjective existence. Of this state of being, groups such as this third group can be the custodian and their problem is therefore:

... To develop that continuity of consciousness which will "open the doors of life and dispel the fear of the known and of that which disappears."   (13-44/5)

PART II

Our ideas about death have been erroneous; we have looked upon it as the great and ultimate terror, whereas in reality it is the great escape, the entrance into a fuller measure of activity, and the release of the life from the crystallised vehicle and an inadequate form.   *(19-64/5)*

PART II

(1)   O*UR SUBJECT now is salvation from the body nature through the process of death. . . .*

Let us first of all define this mysterious process to which all forms are subject and which is frequently only the dreaded end—dreaded because it is not understood. The mind of man is so little developed that fear of the unknown, terror of the unfamiliar, and attachment to form have brought about a situation where one of the most beneficent occurrences in the life cycle of an incarnating Son of God is looked upon as something to be avoided and postponed for as long a time as possible.

Death, if we could but realise it, is one of our most practised activities. We have died many times and shall die again and again. Death is essentially a matter of consciousness. We are conscious one moment on the physical plane, and a moment later we have withdrawn onto another plane and are actively conscious there. Just as long as our consciousness is identified with the form aspect, death will hold for us its ancient terror. Just as soon as we know ourselves to be souls, and find that we are capable of focussing our consciousness or sense of awareness in any form or on any plane at will, or in any direction within the form of God, we shall no longer know death.

Death for the average man is the cataclysmic end, involving the termination of all human relations, the cessation of all physical activity, the severing of all signs of love and of affection, and the passage (unwilling and protesting) into the unknown and the dreaded. It is analogous to leaving a lighted and a warmed room, friendly and familiar, where our loved ones are assembled, and going out into the cold and dark night, alone and terror stricken, hoping for the best and sure of nothing.

But people are apt to forget that every night, in the hours of sleep, we die to the physical plane and are alive and functioning elsewhere. They forget that they have already achieved facility in leaving the physical body; because they cannot as yet bring back

11

into the physical brain consciousness the recollection of that passing out, and of the subsequent interval of active living, they fail to relate death and sleep. Death, after all, is only a longer interval in the life of physical plane functioning; one has only "gone abroad" for a longer period. But the process of daily sleep and the process of occasional dying are identical, with the one difference that in sleep the magnetic thread or current of energy along which the life force streams is preserved intact, and constitutes the path of return to the body. In death, this life thread is broken or snapped. When this has happened, the conscious entity cannot return to the dense physical body and that body, lacking the principle of coherence, then disintegrates.   (4-493/5)

(2)   1. *The Fear of Death* is based upon:
          a. A terror of the final rending processes in the act of death itself.
          b. Horror of the unknown and the indefinable.
          c. Doubt as to final immortality.
          d. Unhappiness at leaving loved ones behind or of being left behind.
          e. Ancient reactions to past violent deaths, lying deep in the subconsciousness.
          f. Clinging to form life, because primarily identified with it in consciousness.
          g. Old erroneous teaching as to Heaven and Hell, both equally unpleasant in prospect to certain types.

    I speak about Death as one who knows the matter from both the outer world experience and the inner life expression:— There is no death. There is, as you know, entrance into fuller life. There is freedom from the handicaps of the fleshly vehicle. The rending process so much dreaded does not exist, except in the cases of violent and sudden death and then the only true disagreeables are an instant and overwhelming sense of imminent peril and destruction, and something closely approaching an electric shock. No more. For the unevolved, death is literally a sleep and a forgetting, for the mind is not sufficiently awakened to react, and the storehouse of memory is as yet practically empty. For the average good citizen, death is a continuance of the living process in his consciousness and a carrying forward of the interests and tendencies of the life. His consciousness and his sense of awareness are the same and unaltered. He does not sense much difference, is well taken care of, and oft is unaware that he has passed through the episode of death. For the wicked and cruelly selfish, for the criminal and for those few who live for the material side only, there eventuates that condition which we call 'earth-bound'. The links they have forged with earth and the earthward bias of all their desires force them to remain close to the earth and their last setting in the earth environment. They seek desperately and by every possible means to re-contact it and to re-enter. In a few cases, great personal love for those left behind or the non-fulfilment of a recognised and urgent duty holds the good and beautiful in a somewhat similar condition. For the aspirant, death is an immediate entrance into a sphere of service and of expression to which he is well accustomed and which he at once recognises as not new. In his sleeping hours he has developed a field of active service and of learning. He now simply functions in it for the entire twenty-four hours (talking in terms of physical plane time) instead of for his usual few hours of earthly sleep.   (4-300/1)

(3)   Another fear which induces mankind to regard death as a calamity is one which theological religion has inculcated, particularly the Protestant fundamentalists and the Roman Catholic Church—the fear of hell, the imposition of penalties, usually out of all proportion to the errors of a lifetime, and the terrors imposed by an angry God. To these man is told he will have to submit, and from them there is no escape, except through the vicarious atonement. There is, as you well know, no angry God, no hell, and no vicarious atonement. There is only a great principle of love animating the entire universe; there is the Presence of the Christ, indicating to humanity the fact of the soul and that we are saved by the livingness of that soul, and the only hell is the earth itself, where we learn to work out our own salvation, actuated by the principle of love and light, and incited thereto by the example of the Christ and the inner urge of our own souls. This teaching anent hell is a remainder of the sadistic turn which was given to the thinking of the Christian Church in the Middle Ages and to the erroneous teaching to be found in the Old Testament anent Jehovah, the tribal God of the Jews. Jehovah is *not* God, the planetary Logos, the Eternal Heart of Love Whom Christ revealed. As these erroneous ideas die out, the concept of hell will fade from man's recollection and its place will be taken by an understanding

of the law which makes each man work out his own salvation upon the physical plane, which leads him to right the wrongs which he may have perpetrated in his lives on Earth, and which enables him eventually to "clean his own slate."

I seek not here to impose upon you a theological discussion. I seek only to point out that the present fear of death must give place to an intelligent comprehension of the reality and to the substitution of a concept of continuity which will negate disturbance, and emphasise the idea of one life and one conscious Entity in many experiencing bodies.   (17-393/4)

(4)   In the coming century, death and the will inevitably will be seen to have new meanings for humanity, and many of the old ideas will vanish. Death, to the average thinking man, is a point of catastrophic crisis. It is the cessation and the ending of all that has been loved, all that is familiar and to be desired; it is a crashing entrance into the unknown, into uncertainty, and the abrupt conclusion of all plans and projects. No matter how much true faith in the spiritual values may be present, no matter how clear the rationalising of the mind may be anent immortality, no matter how conclusive the evidence of persistence and eternity, there still remains a questioning, a recognition of the possibility of complete finality and negation and an end to all activity, or all heart reactions, of all thought, emotion, desire, aspiration, and the intentions which focus around the central core of a man's being. The longing and the determination to persist and the sense of continuity still rest, even to the most determined believer, upon probability, upon an unstable foundation, and upon the testimony of others—who have never in reality returned to tell the truth. The emphasis of all thought on this subject concerns the central "I" or the integrity of Deity.   (18-101/2)

(5)   The *instinct of self-preservation* has its root in an innate fear of death; through the presence of this fear, the race has fought its way to its present point of longevity and endurance. The sciences which concern themselves with the preservation of life, the medical knowledge of the day, and the achievements of civilised comfort have all grown out of this basic fear. All has tended to the persistence of the individual, and to his preserved condition of being. Humanity persists, as a race and as a kingdom in nature, as a result of this fear tendency, this instinctual reaction of the human unit to self-perpetuation.   (4-626)

(6)   I am anxious for you to grasp the teaching I have already given before we proceed to that which is explanatory or new. Study it with care so that the theme of death can more surely and more sanely take shape in your mind. Seek to arrive at a new slant upon the subject and see law and purpose and the beauty of intention in what has hitherto been a terror and a major fear.

Later I shall endeavour to give you some glimpse of the death process as the soul registers it, when undertaking the act of restitution. To you, what I say may appear as speculative or hypothetical; in any case it will be a statement of which few of you will be in a position to prove the accuracy. But surely, brother of mine, it may be more sane and wholesome, more sound and beautiful, than the present darkness and sick hope, and the unhappy speculation and oft despair which overshadows every death bed at this time.   (17-436/7)

PART III

Why not welcome Transition? Learn to glory in experience, which is the gift of wise old age, and look forward to the Great Adventure which confronts you. You know well—in your highest moments—that Transition means realisation without any physical plane limitations. (6-696)

PART III

(1)   THE REASONS why a disciple must at least endeavour not to relax unduly and should push on in spite of fatigue (the fatigue of years of living), in spite of the increasing "creaking" of the human apparatus and the inevitable tendency which comes from constant service and constant contact with others, might be enumerated as follows:

1. He must endeavour to carry the rhythm of service and of fruitful living with him when—free of the physical body—he stands upon the other side of the veil. There must be no gap in that service.
2. He must endeavour as far as in him lies to preserve the continuity of his consciousness as a *working* disciple and should allow no gap to emerge between his present point of tension and that point of tension which supervenes after the death experience.
3. He must endeavour to close the episode of this life experience so that it is apparent that he *is* a member of an Ashram; he must permit no break in the established relationship, or any cessation to the flow of ashramic life through him to the world of men. This activity, on account of the natural and normal deterioration of the physical vehicle as it grows older, is not so easy a task; it requires a definite concentration of effort, thus increasing the tension in which a disciple ever lives. . . .

Disciples in my Ashram have a dual responsibility to stand steady in a *preservation of realisation*—if I may use such a phrase. This steadiness must not be relaxed in any way as old age draws near, and it must not be permitted to disappear through the transition of death itself. It is through the unbroken conscious thinking of a welded group of disciples that the Master of an Ashram works. It is not so much the active outer service of a group of disciples which is of major importance (though it has necessarily a vital purpose) as the coherent, integrated group thought which is so potent in effecting changes in the human consciousness. The peculiar problem of the present world crisis and the terrific readjust-

17

ments in the human consciousness, incident to the inauguration of a new culture, civilisation and world religion, warrant my presenting the members of my Ashram (even affiliated groups, such as yours) with the opportunity to preserve intact and free from all deterioration their "state of mind" throughout the remaining years of this life, through the process of dissolution, and on into the freedom of the other side of the veil. This preservation of conscious integrity is no easy task; it requires understanding and most deliberate effort.   (6-502/4)

(2)   When the true nature of Service is comprehended it will be found that it is an aspect of that divine energy which works always under the destroyer aspect, for it destroys the forms in order to release. Service is a manifestation of the Principle of Liberation, and of this principle, death and service, constitute two aspects. Service saves, liberates and releases, on various levels, the imprisoned consciousness. The same statements can be made of death.   (4-537)

(3)   You will note that I am here dealing with the theme of death as it makes its presence felt through disease or through old age. I am not referring to death as it comes through war or accident, through murder or through suicide. These causes of death, and other causes, come under a totally different directive process; they may not even involve the karma of a man or his individual destiny, as in the case of war. Then vast numbers of people are killed. This has nothing to do with the Law of Cause and Effect as a factor in the soul career of any individual. It is not an act of restitution, planned by a particular soul as it works out its individual destiny. Death, through the destructive processes of war, is under the directive and cyclic intention of the planetary Logos, working through the Council Chamber at Shamballa. The Beings Who there direct world processes know that a time has come when the relation between planetary evil and the Forces of Light or of Good have reached a point of "explosive antagonism" (as it is called). This must be given free rein if the divine purpose is to work out unarrested. The explosion is therefore permitted; nevertheless, all the time a controlling factor is present, even though unrealised by man. Because these Beings (Who work out the will of God) are in no way identified with form life, they have consequently a just appreciation of the relative importance of life in form; the destruction of forms is, to Them, not death in the sense that we under-

stand it, but simply and solely a process of liberation. It is the limited vision of those identified with form which has so consistently nurtured the fear of death. The cycle in which we now live has seen the greatest destruction of human forms in the entire history of our planet. *There has been no destruction of human beings.* I would have you note this statement. Because of this wholesale destruction, humanity has made a very rapid advance towards a more serene attitude in connection with death. This is not yet apparent but—in a few years' time—the new attitude will begin to be marked and the fear of death will begin to die out in the world. This will also be largely due to the increased sensitivity of the human response apparatus, leading to a turning inward or to a new orientation of the human mind, with unpredictable results.

The basis of all wars is fundamentally the sense of separateness. This fundamental individualism or pleased recognition of isolationism leads to all the secondary causes of war: greed, producing economic disaster; hatred, producing national and international friction; cruelty, producing pain and death. The roots of death are therefore deepseated; it is the destruction of the cycle of separateness as an individual upon the physical plane which we call death in the usual sense; consequently death is a process of at-one-ment. Could you but see a little further into the matter, you would learn that death releases the individualised life into a less cramped and confined existence, and eventually—when the death process has been applied to all the three vehicles in the three worlds—into the life of universality. This is a point of inexpressible bliss.   (17-431/3)

(4)   As regards the lengthening of the span of life during the past century of scientific attainment, I would point out that true techniques and the possibilities of organised soul action are always parodied and falsely demonstrated on the physical plane by the earlier scientific activities which are right in motive but which are only a symbol, on the outer sphere of life, of coming and usually future soul action. The life span will eventually be shortened or lengthened at will by souls who consciously serve, and use the mechanism of the body as the instrument whereby the Plan is served. Frequently, today, lives are preserved in form—both in old age and in infancy—that could be well permitted liberation. They serve no useful purpose and cause much pain and suffering to forms which nature (left to herself) would not long use, and would

extinguish. Note that word. Through our overemphasis on the value of form life, and through the universal fear of death—that great transition which we must all face— and through our uncertainty as to the fact of immortality, and also through our deep attachment to form, we arrest the natural processes and hold the life, which is struggling to be free, confined to bodies quite unfitted to the purposes of the soul. Misunderstand me not. I desire to say naught that could place a premium on suicide. But I do say, and I say with emphasis, that the Law of Karma is oft set aside when forms are preserved in coherent expression which should be discarded, for they serve no useful purpose. This preservation is, in the majority of cases, enforced by the subject's group and not by the subject himself—frequently an unconscious invalid, an old person whose response apparatus of contact and response is imperfect, or a baby who is not normal. These cases constitute definite instances of an offsetting of the Law of Karma.   (17-350/1)

PART IV

Disease and death are essentially conditions inherent in sub-stance; just as long as man identifies himself with the form aspect, so will he be conditioned by the Law of Dissolution. This law is a fundamental and natural law governing the life of the form in all the kingdoms of nature.   (17-501)

PART IV

(1) THE RELEASE of a soul through disease and death is not necessarily an unhappy occurrence. A new and better attitude to the phenomenon of death is essential, is possible and near. Upon this I need not here enlarge. But I do seek to give you a new slant on the subject of sickness and of death.   (17-350)

(2)   Second, disease is sometimes incident upon and part of the process of the withdrawal of the soul from its habitation. This we call death, and it can come quickly and unexpectedly when the soul withdraws with suddeness from its body. Or death can spread itself over a long period of time, and the soul may take several months or years for its slow and gradual emergence from the body, with the body dying by inches all the time.   (17-41)

(3)   Disease can be a gradual and slow process of dying and of thus releasing the soul. A cure then will not be possible, though palliative and ameliorative measures are needed and should most certainly be used. The length of the life can be prolonged, but a permanent and final cure is out of the question. This the average mental healer fails to realise. They make a horror out of death, whereas death is a beneficent friend.

Disease can be the sudden and final call to the body to relinquish the soul and set it free for other service.

In all these cases everything possible should be done from the standpoint of modern medical and surgical science and the allied sciences of which there are today so many. Much too can be done from the angle of mental and spiritual healing, aided by the science of psychology. Some day there must come cooperation in these various fields and a synthesising of their efforts.   (17-42)

(4)   It will be apparent to the casual thinker that many diseases and many causes of death are due to environing conditions for which he is in no way responsible. These range all the way from purely external occurrences to hereditary predispositions. They might be listed as follows:

23

1. *Accidents,* which may be due to personal negligence, group happenings, the carelessness of other people, and the results of fighting, as in labour strikes or war. They can also be brought about by attacks from the animal or the snake world, accidental poisonings and many other causes.
2. *Infections* coming to a man from outside and not as the result of his own peculiar blood condition. Such infections are the various so-called infectious and contagious diseases, and prevalent epidemics. These may come to a man in the line of duty, through his daily contacts, or through a widespread condition of disease in his environment.
3. *Diseases due to malnutrition,* particularly when found in the young. This state of undernourishment predisposes the body to disease, lowers the resistance and the vitality, and offsets the "fighting powers" of the man, leading to premature death.
4. *Heredity.* There are, as you well know, ceratin forms of hereditary weaknesses, which either predispose a person to certain illnesses and consequent death, or produce in him those conditions which lead to a steady weakening of his hold on life; there are also those tendencies which constitute a form of dangerous appetite, which lead to undesirable habits, a letting down of the morale, and are dangerous to the will of the person, rendering him futile to fight these predispositions. He succumbs to them and pays the price of such habits, which is disease and death.　　(17-18/9)

(5)　　　　There are one or two things which I would like to make clear and which you must, in your turn, make clear to the patient.

1. Cure is not guaranteed. Patients must realise that continuance of life in the physical body is not the highest possible goal. It may be so if the service to be rendered is of real import, if obligations remain still to be carried out, and if other lessons must still be learned. Bodily existence is not, however, the summum bonum of existence. Freedom from the limitations of the physical body is of real beneficence. Patients must learn to recognise and accept the Law of Karma.
2. Fear is needless. One of the first objectives of the healing agent should be to aid the patient to achieve a happy, sane, expectant outlook upon his future—no matter what the future may bring.　　(17-387)

(6)   Therefore, the healer has the duty of rendering himself effective, and according to what he is, so will be the effect upon the patient. When a healer works magnetically and radiates his soul force to the patient, that patient is enabled more easily to achieve the end desired—which may be complete healing, or it may be the establishing of a state of mind which will enable the patient to live with himself and with his complaint, unhandicapped by the karmic limitations of the body. Or it may be enabling the patient to achieve (with joy and facility) the right liberation from the body and, through the portal of death, to pass to complete health.   (17-8)

(7)   Various cultists and healers usually take the position that it is of major importance that the physical vehicle be rendered free from disease and clutched away from the processes of death. It might, however, be desirable (and it often is) that the disease be permitted to do its work and death open the door to the escape of the soul from imprisonment. The time comes inevitably to all incarnated beings when the soul demands liberation from the body and from form life, and nature has her own wise ways of doing this. Disease and death must be recognised as liberating factors when they come as the result of right timing by the soul. It must be realised by students that the physical form is an aggregate of atoms, built into organisms and finally into a coherent body, and that this body is held together by the will of the soul. Withdraw that will on to its own plane or (as it is occultly expressed) "let the soul's eye turn in another direction" and, in this present cycle, disease and death will inevitably supervene. This is not mental error, or failure to recognise divinity, or succumbing to evil. It is, in reality, the resolution of the form nature into its component parts and basic essence. Disease is essentially an aspect of death. It is the process by which the material nature and the substantial form prepares itself for separation from the soul.   (17-111)

(8)   Nobody is ever brought back from the "gates of death" whose karma indicates that his time has come; the life cycle on the physical plane then ends unless he is a worker in an Ashram, a disciple of some standing whose work and presence is still needed on earth to complete his assigned task. Then the master of the Ashram may add His knowledge and energy to that of the healer or to that of the patient, and bring about a temporary

postponement of departure. Upon this the healer may not count, or the patient either, for they know not the full and warranting circumstances.   (17-704)

(9)   Where death is definitely indicated and the "signs of death" are noted by both the doctor and the healer, the healer has not need to stop his work. By continuing it, he may increase the evil condition, but will nevertheless be aiding the patient by hastening normally the act of dying. The old proverb is basically not true in all cases, that "where there is life there is hope." Life can and often is prolonged after the will of the soul is towards the withdrawal of the soul life; the life of the atoms of the lunar lords can be fostered for a long time, and this greatly distresses the spiritual man who is aware of the process and the intent of his soul. What is kept alive is the physical body, but the interest of the true man is no longer focussed there.

There inevitably comes a point, for instance in the case of malignant disease, where the physician knows that it simply is a question of time, and the spiritual healer can learn to recognise the same signs. Then, instead of the present silence on the part of both healer and doctor, where the patient is concerned, this remaining time will be employed (if the patient's faculties permit) with due preparation for the "beneficent and happy withdrawal" of the soul; the patient's family and friends will share in the preparation. In the early stages of the new world religion, this attitude towards death will be inculcated. An entirely new concept of death, with the emphasis upon conscious withdrawal, will be taught, and funeral services, or rather the crematory services, will be joyous events because their emphasis will be upon release and return.   (17-652/3)

(10)   If I were asked to say what is the major task of all healing groups, such as the Hierarchy seeks to see functioning in the future, I would say it is to prepare human beings for what we should regard as the restorative aspect of death, and thus give to that hitherto dreaded enemy of mankind a new and happier significance. You will find that if you work along these indicated lines of thought, the entire theme of death will constantly recur, and that the result of this will be new attitudes to dying and the inculcation of a happy expectancy where that inevitable and most familiar event occurs. Healing groups must prepare to deal with this basic

conditon of all living, and a major part of their work will be the elucidating of the principle of death. The soul, we are told, must return to the one who gave it. To date that has been an enforced and dreaded restitution, one which engenders fear and which leads men and women everywhere to clamour for the healing of the physical body, overemphasising its importance and making them regard the prolongation of earthly existence as the most important factor in their lives. During the next cycle, these wrong attitudes must come to an end; death will become a normal and understood process—as normal as the process of birth, though evoking less pain and fear. This comment of mine is in the nature of a prophecy and should be noted as such.   (17-389/90)

PART V

There is a technique of dying just as there is of living . . . .
(4-302)

PART V

(1)   THERE IS a big difference now between the scientific method of bringing people into incarnation and the perfectly blind and oft frightened and surely ignorant way in which we usher them out of incarnation. I seek today to open the door in the occident to a newer and more scientific method of handling the process of dying, and let me make myself perfectly clear. What I have to say in no way abrogates modern medical science with its palliatives and skill. All I plead for is a sane approach to death; all I seek to make is a suggestion that when pain has worn itself out and weakness has supervened, the dying person be permitted to prepare himself, even if apparently unconscious, for the great transition. Forget not that it takes strength and a strong hold on the nervous apparatus to produce pain. Is it impossible to conceive of a time when the act of dying will be a triumphant finale of life? Is it impossible to vision the time when the hours spent on the death bed may be but a glorious prelude to a conscious exit? When the fact that the man is to discard the handicap of the physical sheath may be for him and those around him the long waited for and joyous consummation? Can you not visualize the time when instead of tears and fear and the refusal to recognize the inevitable, the dying person and his friends would mutually agree on the hour and that nothing but happiness would characterize the passing? That in the minds of those left behind the thought of sorrow will not enter and death beds will be regarded as happier occasions than births and marriages? I tell you, that before so very long this will be deeply so for the intelligent of the race, and little by little for all.

You say there are as yet only beliefs as to immortality and no sure evidences. In the accumulation of testimony, in the inner assurances of the human heart, in the fact of belief in eternal persistence as an idea in the minds of men lies sure indication. But indication will give place to conviction and knowledge before another hundred years has elapsed, for an event will take place and a revelation be given to the race which will turn hope into certainty and belief into knowledge. In the meantime, let a new attitude to death be cultivated and a new science of death be inaugurated. Let it cease to be the one thing we cannot control and which inevitably defeats us and let us begin to control our passing over to the other side, and to understand somewhat the technique of transition.   (4-499/500)

(2)   We are therefore considering, in this second section, the problem of death or the art of dying. This is something which all seriously ill people must inevitably face, and for which those in good health should prepare themselves through correct thinking and sane anticipation. The morbid attitude of the majority of men to the subject of death, and their refusal to consider it when in good health, is something which must be altered and deliberately changed. Christ demonstrated to His disciples the correct attitude when referring to His coming and immediate decease at the hand of His enemies; He chided them when they evidenced sorrow, reminding them that He was going to His Father. Being an initiate of high degree, He meant that He was, occultly speaking, "making restitution to the Monad"; ordinary people and those below the grade of an initiate of the third degree make "restitution to the soul."   (17-391/2)

(3)   The reign of the fear of death is well-nigh ended and we shall soon enter upon a period of knowledge and of certainty which will cut away the ground from under all our fears. In dealing with the fear of death, there is little to be done except to raise the whole subject onto a more scientific level, and—in this scientific sense—teach people to die. There is a technique of dying just as there is of living, but this technique has been lost very largely in the West and is almost lost except in a few centres of Knowers in the East.   (4-302)

(4)   The second point to be grasped is that there can be a technique of dying and a training given during life which will lead up to the utilization of that technique.

        As regards the training to which a man can submit himself I will give a few hints which will be found to convey a new meaning to much work now being done by all aspirants. The Elder Brothers of the race who have guided humanity through long centuries, are now busy preparing people for the next great step to be taken.

This step will bring in a continuity of consciousness which will do away with all fear of death and link the physical and astral planes in such a close relation that they will in reality constitute one plane. Just as an at-one-ment has to be brought about between the various aspects of man, so a similar unification has to take place in connection with the various aspects of the planetary life. The planes have to be at-one-ed as well as soul and body. This has already been largely accomplished between the etheric plane and the dense physical plane. Now it is being rapidly carried forward between the physical and the astral.

In the work being done by seekers in all departments of human thought and life, this unification is proceeding and in the training now suggested to earnest and sincere aspirants, there are other objectives than just the one of producing soul and body at-one-ment. No emphasis, however, is laid upon them, owing to the ability of man unduly to emphasize the wrong objectives. It might well be asked if it is possible to give a simple set of rules that could be followed now by all who seek to establish such a rhythm that life itself is not only organized and constructive, but when the moment for vacating the outer sheath arrives, there will be no problem nor difficulty. I will, therefore, give you four simple rules that link up with much that all students are now doing:

1. Learn to keep focussed in the head through visualization and meditation and through the steady practice of concentration; develop the capacity to live increasingly as the king seated on the throne between the eyebrows. This is a rule that can be applied to the every day affairs of life.
2. Learn to render heart service and not an emotional insistence on activity directed towards handling the affairs of others. This involves, prior to all such activity, the answering of two questions: — Am I rendering this service to an individual as an individual, or am I rendering it as a member of a group to a group? Is my motive an egoic impulse, or am I prompted by emotion, ambition to shine and love of being loved or admired? These two activities will result in the focussing of the life energies above the diaphragm and so negate the attractive power of the solar plexus. Hence, that centre will become increasingly inactive and there will not be so much danger of puncturing the web in that locality.

3. Learn, as you go to sleep, to withdraw the consciousness to the head. This should be practiced as a definite exercise as one falls to sleep. One should not permit oneself to drift off to sleep, but should endeavor to preserve the consciousness intact until there is a conscious passing out onto the astral plane. Relaxation, close attention, and a steady drawing upwards to the center in the head should be attempted, for until the aspirant has learned to be steadily aware of all processes in going to sleep and to preserve at the same time his positivity, there is danger in this work. The first steps must be taken with intelligence and followed for many years until facility in the work of abstraction is achieved.

4. Record and watch all phenomena connected with the withdrawing process, whether followed in the meditation work or in going to sleep. It will be found, for instance, that many people wake with an almost painful start just as they have dropped asleep. This is due to the slipping out of the consciousness through a web which is not adequately clear and through an orifice which is partially closed. Others may hear an intensely loud snap in the region of the head. This is caused by the vital airs in the head of which we are not usually aware and is produced by an inner aural sensitivity which causes awareness of sounds always present but not usually registered. Others will see light as they fall asleep, or clouds of color, or banners and streamers of violet, all of which are etheric phenomena. These phenomena which are of no real moment, are all related to the vital body, to pranic emanations, and to the web of light.

The carrying on of this practice and the following of these four rules over a period of years will do much to facilitate the technique of the death bed, for the man who has learned to handle his body as he falls asleep, has an advantage over the man who never pays any attention to the process.

In relation to the technique of dying it is only possible for me at this time to make one or two suggestions. I deal not here with the attitude of the attendant watchers, I deal only with those points which will make for an easier passing over of the transient soul.

First, let there be silence in the chamber. This is, of course, frequently the case. It must be remembered that the dying person may usually be unconscious. This unconsciousness is apparent but not real. In nine hundred cases out of a thousand the brain awareness is there, with a full consciousness of happenings, but there is a complete paralysis of the will to express and complete inability to generate the energy which will indicate aliveness. When silence and understanding rule the sick room, the departing soul can hold possession of its instrument with clarity until the last minute and can make due preparation.

Later, when more anent color is known, only orange lights will be permitted in the sick room of a dying person, and these will only be installed with due ceremony when there is assuredly no possibility of recovery. Orange aids the focussing in the head, just as red stimulates the solar plexus and green has a definite effect upon the heart and life streams

Certain types of music will be used when more in connection with sound is understood, but there is no music as yet which will facilitate the work of the soul in abstracting itself from the body, though certain notes on the organ will be found effective. At the exact moment of death, if a person's own note is sounded, it will coordinate the two streams of energy and eventually rupture the life thread, but the knowledge of this is too dangerous to transmit yet and can only later be given. I would indicate the future and the lines along which future occult study will run.

It will be found also that pressure on certain nerve centers and on certain arteries will facilitate the work. (This science of dying is held in custody, as many students know, in Tibet.) Pressure on the jugular vein and on certain big nerves in the region of the head and on a particular spot in the medulla oblongata will be found helpful and effective. A definite science of death will inevitably later be elaborated, but only when the fact of the soul is recognized and its relation to the body has been scientifically demonstrated.

Mantric phrases will also be employed and definitely built into the consciousness of the dying person by those around him, or employed deliberately and mentally by himself. The Christ demonstrated their use when he cried aloud, "Father, into Thy hands I commend my spirit." And we have another instance in the words, "Lord, now lettest Thou Thy servant depart in peace." The steady use of the Sacred Word chanted in an undertone or on a particular key (to which the dying man will be found to respond) may later constitute also a part of the ritual of transition accompanied by the anointing with oil, as preserved in the Catholic Church. Extreme

unction has an occult, scientific basis. The top of the head of the
dying man should also symbolically point towards the East and the
feet and the hands should be crossed. Sandalwood only should be
burned in the room and no incense of any other kind permitted, for
sandalwood is the incense of the first or destroyer ray and the soul
is in process of destroying its habitation.

This is all I can at this time communicate on the subject
of death for the consideration of the general public. But I con-
jure all of you to push the study of death and its technique as
far as possible and to carry forward occult investigation of this
matter.   (4-502/7)

(5)   To resume with your own instruction, if you would care
to increase the capacity of the three activities—contact, impression,
relationship—you might follow a simple exercise when going to
sleep at night.

After achieving complete comfort, as far as may be possible,
attempt to assume an inner attitude of planned, quiet discarding of
the physical body, keeping the whole concept upon the mental
plane, yet realising it to be a simple brain activity. The heart is in
no way to be involved. Your objective is to preserve consciousness
as you withdraw it from the brain and pass out on the subtler
levels of awareness. You are *not* discarding the physical body
permanently, therefore the life thread anchored in the heart is not
involved. The aim is, for a few hours and whilst clothed in the
astral and mental vehicles, to be *consciously* aware elsewhere.
With determination you become a focussed, interested point of
consciousness, intent on emerging from the casing of the physical
body. That point you hold, refusing to look backward at the physical vehicle, or at the worries, interests and circumstances of daily
life, fixedly waiting for the moment when your negative attitude to
the physical plane and your positive attitude to the inner planes
will bring a moment of release, perhaps a flash of light, the perception of an aperture of escape, or the recognition of your surroundings, plus the elimination of all surprise or the expectation
of any phenomena.

You are (as you practice this exercise of withdrawal) only
going through an ordinary everyday process. If facility in doing
this exercise is achieved, the hour of death will find you automatically and easily—because the physical body is making no resistance but remains quiescent and negative—able to make the Great

Transition without concern or fear of the unknown. This is an exercise I would like to see all the group undertake. It involves only the steady preservation of an attitude, a fixed determination to hold on to the point of consciousness which is your persistent Self, plus a live expectancy. I have chosen these words with care and would ask you to study them with equal care.   (6-488/9)

PART VI

. . . [People] fail to relate death and sleep. Death, after all, is only a longer interval in the life of physical plane functioning; one has only "gone abroad" for a longer period. (4-495)

PART VI

(1)   F̲OR THE̲ unevolved, death is literally a sleep and a forgetting, for the mind is not sufficiently awakened to react, and the storehouse of memory is as yet practically empty.   (4-300)

(2)   For the average good citizen, death is a continuance of the living process in his consciousness and a carrying forward of the interests and tendencies of the life. His consciousness and his sense of awareness are the same and unaltered.   (4-300)

(3)   You must always bear in mind that the consciousness remains the same whether in physical incarnation or out of incarnation, and that development can be carried on with even greater ease than when limited and conditioned by the brain consciousness.   (5-81)

(4)   With the mass of ordinary humanity, focused in all their activities and their thinking upon the physical plane, the period after death is one of semi-consciousness, of a failure to recognize location, and of emotional and mental bewilderment. With disciples there is still contact with people (usually those with whom they have been associated) in the hours of sleep; there is still the reception of impression from environment and associates, and there is still the recognition of relation with (as on earth) the assumption of responsibility.   (6-487/8)

(5)   Therefore, taking the average man, what are his first reactions and activities after the restitution of the physical body to the universal reservoir of substance? Let me enumerate some of these reactions:

1. He becomes consciously aware of himself. This involves a clarity of perception unknown to the average man whilst in physical incarnation.
2. Time (being the succession of events as registered by the physical brain) is now nonexistent as we understand the term, and—as the man turns his attention to his more clearly defined

37

emotional self—there ensues *invariably* a moment of direct soul contact. This is due to the fact that even in the case of the most ignorant and undeveloped man, the moment of complete restitution does not pass unnoticed by the soul. It has a definite soul effect, something like a long and strong pull at a bell rope, if I might use so simple a simile. For a brief second the soul responds, and the nature of the response is such that the man, standing in his astral body, or rather in his kama-manasic vehicle, sees the experience of the past incarnation spread before him like a map. He records a sense of timelessness.

3. As a result of the recognition of these experiences, the man isolates those three which were the three major conditioning factors in the life which has gone and which also hold the keys to his future incarnation which he will next initiate. All else is forgotten, and all the lesser experiences fade out of his memory, leaving nothing in his consciousness but what are esoterically called "the three seeds or germs of the future." These three seeds are in a peculiar manner related to the permanent physical and astral atoms, and thus produce the fivefold force which will create the forms later to appear. It might be said that:

   a. *Seed One* determines later the nature of the physical environment in which the returning man will find his place. It is related to the quality of that future environment and thus conditions the needed field or area of contact.

   b. *Seed Two* determines the quality of the etheric body as a vehicle through which the ray forces can make contact with the dense physical body. It delimits the etheric structure or vital web along which the incoming energies will circulate and is related in particular to the special one of the seven centres which will be the most active and alive during the coming incarnation.

   c. *Seed Three* gives the key to the astral vehicle in which the man will be polarised in the next incarnation. Forget not, I am dealing here with the average man and not with the advanced human being, disciple or initiate. It is this seed which—through the forces it attracts—brings the man again into relation with those he previously loved or with whom he had close contact. It can be accepted as a fact that the group idea governs subjectively all incarnations, and that reincarnated man is brought into incarnation not only through his own desire for physical plane experience, but also under group impulse and in line with the group karma as well as with his own. This is a point which should receive more emphasis. Once this is truly grasped and understood, a great deal of the fear engendered by the thought of death would disappear. The familiar and the loved will still remain the familiar and the loved, because the relation has been closely established over many incarnations and—as the *Old Commentary* expresses it:

"These seeds of determining recognition are not unique to me and you, but also for the group; within the group they relate one to the other in time and space. Only in the lower three shall those related find their true existence. When soul knows soul and in the meeting-place within the Master's call, these seeds shall disappear."

It will be apparent, therefore, how necessary it is to train children to recognize and profit by experience, for this, once learnt, will greatly facilitate this third activity upon the astral plane after death.

4. Having completed this "isolating of experience," the man will then seek and automatically find those whom the third seed influence indicates as possessing a constant part in the group experience of which he is an element, consciously or unconsciously. The relation once again established (if those sought have not yet eliminated the physical body), the man acts as he would on earth in the company of his intimates and according to his temperament and point in evolution. If those who are closest to him and whom he deeply loves or hates are still in physical incarnation, he will also seek them out and—just again as he did on earth—he will remain in their neighborhood, aware of their activities, though (unless highly evolved) they will not be aware of his. I can give no detail as to reciprocal give and take or to the modes and methods of contact. Each person differs; each temperament is largely unique. I only seek to make clear certain basic lines of behavior pursued by man prior to the act or acts of elimination.

These four activities cover varying periods of time—from the angle of "those who live below," though there is no time recognised on the part of the man on the astral plane. Gradually the lure and glamour (of a low or high order) wears off, and the man enters into tage where he *knows* — because the mind is now more incisive and dominating — that he is ready for the second death and for the entire elimination of the kamic body or of the kama-manasic vehicle.   (17-491/4)

(6)   Immediately after death, and particularly if cremation has taken place, the man, in his kama-manasic body, is as much aware and alert to his environment as he was upon the physical plane when alive. This phrasing permits latitude as to the extent of the awareness and of observation, for a similar latitude must be allowed for those on the physical plane. People are not all equally awake or equally conscious of circumstances or immediate experience. However, as most people are more conscious emotionally than they are physically, and live to a great extent focussed in their astral vehicles, the man is quite familiar with the state of consciousness in which he finds himself. Forget not that a plane is essentially a state of consciousness and *not* a locality, as so many esotericists seem to think. It is recognized by the focussed reaction of the self-conscious person who — constantly and distinctly aware of himself — is sentient to the theme of his environment and of his outgoing desires, or (where advanced people are concerned, functioning upon the more advanced levels of the astral plane) sentient of outgoing love and aspiration; the man is engrossed with what engrossed his attention and involved the kamic principle during his incarnated experience. May I again remind you that there is now no physical brain to respond to impacts generated by the inner man, and also that sex, as it is physically understood, is nonexistent. Spiritualists would do well to remember this and so grasp the foolishness as well as the impossibility of those spiritual marriages which certain schools of thought in the movement teach and practice. The man, in his astral body, is now free from the strictly animal impulses which, upon the physical plane, are both normal and right, but which now have no meaning to him in his kamic body.   (17-490/1)

(7)   In considering the consciousness of the departing soul (note that phrase) as it undertakes the act of restitution, I would again point out that I am dealing with a subject of which there is no tangible physical proof. Occasionally men are brought back again into physical plane existence when at the exact point of complete physical restitution. This can only be done as long as the conscious entity is still occupying the etheric vehicle, though the

discarding of the dense physical body has to all intents and purposes been completed. Though the etheric body interpenetrates the entire physical body, it is much larger than that body, and the astral body and the mental nature can still remain etherically polarised even if the death of the physical body—the cessation of all heart activity and the concentration of the basic etheric focus in the region of the head, or the heart, or the solar plexus—has been effective and the withdrawal is already well under way.   (17-460)

(8)   From the moment of complete separation from the dense physical and etheric bodies, and as the eliminative process is undertaken, the man is *aware of past and present;* when elimination is complete and the hour of soul contact eventuates and the manasic vehicle is in process of destruction, he becomes immediately *aware of the future,* for prediction is an asset of the soul consciousness and in this the man temporarily shares. Therefore, past, present and future are seen as one; the recognition of the Eternal Now is gradually developed from incarnation to incarnation and during the continuous process of rebirth. This constitutes a state of consciousness (characteristic of the normal state of the advanced man) which can be called devachanic.   (17-496/7)

(9)   For the aspirant, death is an immediate entrance into a sphere of service and of expression to which he is well accustomed and which he at once recognizes as not new.   (4-301)

(10)   It is not my intention to elaborate the technique of the eliminative process. Humanity is at so many different stages— intermediate between the three already outlined—that it would be impossible to be definite or concise. Attrition is relatively easy to understand; the kamic body dies out because, there being no call from physical substance, evoking desire, there is nothing with which to feed this vehicle. The astral body comes into being through the reciprocal interplay between the physical plane, which is not a principle, and the principle of desire; in the process of taking rebirth, this principle is utilized with dynamic intent by the soul in the mental vehicle to reverse the call, and matter then responds to the call of the reincarnating man. Kamic man, after a long process of attrition, is left standing free within an embryonic mental vehicle, and this period of semi-mental life is exceedingly brief and is brought to an end by the soul who suddenly "directs his eye to the waiting one," and by the power of that directed potency instantaneously reorients the individual kamic man to the downward path of

rebirth. The kama-manasic man practices a process of withdrawal and responds to the "pull" of a rapidly developing mental body. This withdrawal becomes increasingly rapid and dynamic until it reaches the state where the probationary disciplie—under steadily growing soul contact—shatters the kama-manasic body, as a unit, by an act of the mental will, implemented by the soul. You will note that the "devachanic" experience will necessarily be briefer in connection with this majority than with the kamic minority, because the devachanic technique of review and recognition of the implications of experience is slowly controlling the man on the physical plane so that he brings the significance of meaning and learns constantly through experience whilst incarnating. Thus you will realize also that continuity of consciouness is also being slowly developed, and the awarenesses of the inner man begin to demonstrate on the physical plane, through the medium of the physical brain at first, and then independently of that material structure. I have here conveyed a definite hint on a subject which will receive wide attention during the next two hundred years.

The manasic person, the integrated personality, works, as we have seen, in two ways which are necessarily dependent upon the integration achieved. This integration will be of two kinds:

1. That of the integrated personality focussed in the mind and achieving a constantly growing rapport with the soul.
2. The disciple, whose integrated personality is now being rapidly integrated into and absorbed by the soul.

In this stage of mind development and of constant mental control (based on the fact that the man's consciousness is now definitely focussed and permanently centered in the mental vehicle), the earlier processes of the destruction of the astral body through attrition and by "dynamic negation" are carried on whilst in physical incarnation. The incarnated man refuses to be ruled by desire; what is left of the illusory astral body is dominated now by the mind, and the urges towards the satisfaction of desire are refused with full and conscious deliberation, either because of the selfish ambitions and mental intentions of the integrated personality, or under the inspiration of soul intention which subordinates the mind to its purposes. When this point in evolution is attained, the man can then dissolve the last remaining vestiges of all desire by means of *illumination.* In the early stages of purely manasic or mental life, this is done through the illumination which knowledge brings and involves mainly the innate light of mental substance. Later, when soul and mind are establishing a close rapport, the light of the soul hastens and supplements the process. The disciple now uses more occult methods, but upon these I may not here enlarge. The destruction of the mental body is no longer brought about by the destructive power of light itself, but is hastened by means of certain sounds, emanating from the plane of the spiritual will; these are recognized by the disciple, and permission to use them in their proper word-forms is given to him by some senior initiate within the Ashram or by the Master Himself, towards the close of the cycle of incarnation.   (17-497/9)

(11)   We come now to the enunciation of a new law which is substituted for the Law of Death and which has reference only to those upon the later stages of the Path of Discipleship and the stages upon the Path of Initiation.

LAW X

Hearken, O Chela, to the call which comes from the Son to. the Mother, and then obey. The Word goes forth that form has served its purpose. The principle of mind (the fifth principle. A.A.B.) then organizes itself, and then repeats the Word. The waiting form responds and drops away. The soul stands free.

Respond, O Rising One, to the call which comes within the sphere of obligation; recognize the call emerging from the Ashram or from the Council Chamber where waits the Lord of Life Himself. The Sound goes forth. Both soul and form together must renounce the principle of life and thus permit the Monad to stand free. The soul responds. The form then shatters the connection. Life is now liberated, owning the quality of conscious knowledge and the fruit of all experience. These are the gifts of soul and form combined.

I have wished to make clear in your minds the distinction between disease and death as experienced by the average man, and certain corresponding processes of conscious dissolution as practised by the advanced disciple or initiate. These later processes involve a slowly developing technique in which (in the earlier stages) the disciple is still the victim of disease-producing tendencies of the form, as of all forms in nature. This tendency produces subsequent death, through the stages of modified disease and peaceful, consequent death, on to the other stages where death is brought about by an act of the will—the time and the mode being determined by the soul and consciously recorded and registered in the brain. Pain is demonstrated in both cases, but upon the Path of Initiation pain is largely negated, not because the initiate endeavours to avoid pain, but because the sensitivity of the form to undesirable contacts disappears, and with it pain also disappears; pain is the guardian of the form and the protector of substance; it warns of danger; it indicates certain definite stages in the evolutionary process; it is related to the principle whereby the soul identifies itself with substance. When the identification ceases, pain and disease and also death lose their hold upon the disciple; the soul is no longer subject to their requirements, and the man is free because disease and death are qualities inherent in form, and subject to the vicissitudes of form life.   (17-501/2)

PART VII

. . . death can be best regarded as the experience which frees us from the illusion of form . . . . *(22-243)*

PART VII

(1) $\quad$ T HE TIBETANS speak of the process of death as that of "entering into the clear cold light." It is possible that death can be best regarded as the experience which frees us from the illusion of form; and this brings clearly to our minds the realisation that when we speak of death we are referring to a process which concerns the material nature, the body, with its psychical faculties and its mental processes. $\quad$ (22-243)

(2) $\quad$ [Man's] error at this time consists in ... his attitude to death, and his feeling that the disappearance of the life out of visual perception through the medium of form, and the consequent disintegration of that form, indicates disaster. $\quad$ (17-13)

(3) $\quad$ The destruction of form in battle (which causes so much fear to many of you) is of small importance to those who *know* that reincarnation is a basic law of nature and that *there is no death.* The forces of death are abroad today, but it is the death of liberty, the death of free speech, the death of freedom in human action, the death of truth and of the higher spiritual values *These* are the vital factors in the life of humanity; the death of the physical form is a negligible factor in relation to these, and one easily righted again through the processes of rebirth and fresh opportunity. $\quad$ (13-232)

(4) $\quad$ Students are apt to think that death ends things, whereas from the angle of *termination* we are dealing with values which are persistent, with which there is no interference, nor can there be any, and which hold within themselves the seeds of immortality. I would have you ponder on this and know that everything that is of true spiritual value is persistent, ageless, immortal and eternal. Only that dies which is valueless, and—from the standpoint of humanity—that means those factors which emphasise and assume importance where the form is concerned. But those values which are based on principle and not upon the detail of appearance have in them that undying principle which leads a man from the

"gates of nativity, through the gates of perception, to the gates of purpose"—as the *Old Commentary* expresses it.   (17-684)

(5)   Death and limitation are synonymous terms. When the consciousness is focussed in form and identified entirely with the principle of limitation, it regards freedom from form life as death; but, as evolution proceeds, the consciousness shifts increasingly into awareness of that which is *not* form and into the realm of that which is transcendent or into the world of the abstract, i.e., into that which is abstracted from form and focussed in itself. This, by the way, is a definition of meditation from the angle of goal and achievement. A man can truly meditate when he begins to use the mind, the reflection of the will aspect, and employs it in its three aspects: as initiating his entrance into the world of souls, as conditioning his personality life and as enforcing and eventually bringing about a full expression of soul purpose. This results in the complete overcoming of death.   (16-615/6)

(6)   Death itself is a part of the great illusion and only exists because of the veils which we have gathered around ourselves.   (5-463)

(7)   Fear of death and depression constitute for man the Dweller on the Threshold in this age and cycle. Both of them indicate sentient reaction to psychological factors and cannot be dealt with by the use of another factor such as courage. They must be met by the omniscience of the soul, working through the mind—not by its omnipotence. In this is to be found an occult hint.   (17-443)

(8)   The preparation for this kingdom is the task of discipleship and constitutes the arduous discipline of the five-fold way of initiation. The work of the disciple is the founding of the kingdom, and the primary characteristic of its citizens is immortality. They are members of a Deathless Race, and the final enemy which they overcome is death; they function consciously in or out of the body and care not which it is; they have life everlasting because there is in them that which cannot die, being of the nature of God.   (22-276)

PART VIII

... death is only an interlude in a life of steadily accumulating experience ... it marks a definite transition from one <u>state of consciousness into another.</u>   *(22-242)*

PART VIII

(1) DEATH IS in reality unconsciousness of that which may be functioning in some form or another, but in a form of which the spiritual entity is totally unaware.   (17-445)

(2)   Death is essentially a matter of consciousness. We are conscious one moment on the physical plane, and a moment later we have withdrawn onto another plane and are actively conscious there.   (4-494)

(3)   In the case of initiates, it is somewhat different, because they frequently remain fully conscious through the death process.   (17-540)

(4)   ... the destruction of forms is, to Them, not death in the sense that we understand it, but simply and solely a process of liberation.   (17-432)

(5)   The soul, through alignment, enters into a right use of time; or rather the brain, which is the only time-conscious factor in man, is no longer the dominant attribute; the mind, as the agent of the soul (whose consciousness is inclusive of the past, present, and the future), sees life and experience as it truly is. Death, therefore, is referred to as an episode, and as a transitional point in a vast series of transitions. When this attitude of the soul is grasped, our entire technique of living, and incidentally of dying, is utterly altered.   (17-351)

(6)   ... we shall regard death as only another step on the way towards light and life. ...   (22-233)

(7)   ... in the later stages of life, we have the crystallisation of the form, and the man's realisation of its inadequacy. Then comes the happy release which we call death, that great moment in which the "spirit in prison" escapes from the confining walls of its physical form.   (19-64)

(8)   I refer here to death as the Great Releaser, which shatters the forms which are bringing death to that which is embodied.   (16-545)

(9)   . . . death is a great Liberator.   (18-607)

(10)   Frequently I have told you that the Hierarchy works only with the spiritual nature or with the soul of humanity, and that—to the Master—the form is regarded as relatively of no importance. Release from the three-fold form is ever regarded by the spiritual man as the greatest possible good, provided it comes to him under law, as the result of his spiritual destiny and of karmic decision; it must not come as an arbitrary act, or as an escape from life and its consequences upon the physical plane, or as self-imposed.   (17-661)

(11)   It is interesting here to note that death is governed by the Principle of Liberation, and not by that of Limitation. Death is only recognised as a factor to be dealt with by self-conscious lives and is only misunderstood by human beings, who are the most glamoured and deluded of all incarnated lives.   (4-534)

(12)   Death . . . is simply the Bringer of Changes.

(22-241/2)

(13)   . . . death itself is a part of the creative process of synthesising.   (17-680)

(14)   I speak about Death as one who knows the matter from both the outer world experience and the inner life expression: —There is no death. There is, as you know, entrance into fuller life.   (4-300)

(15)   The Law of Death and Sacrifice governs the gradual disintegration of concrete forms and their sacrifice to the evolving life . . . .   (17-414)

(16)   The Law of Sacrifice and Death is the controlling factor on the physical plane. The destruction of the form, in order that the evolving life may progress, is one of the fundamental methods in evolution.   (17-413)

(17)   A Master learns the meaning of each confining form; then He assumes control and wields the law upon the plane consistent with the form. He has then outgrown the form and discards it for other and higher forms. Thus, He has progressed always by means of the sacrifice and death of the form. Always, it is recognised as imprisoning, always it must be sacrificed and die so that the life within may speed ever on and up. The path of resurrection

presupposes crucifixion and death, and then leads to the mount whence Ascension may be made.   (17-459/60)

(18)   The whole must be seen as of more vital importance than the part, and this not as a dream, a vision, a theory, a process of wishful thinking, a hypothesis or an urge. It is realised as an innate necessity and as inevitable. It connotes death, but death as beauty, as joy, as spirit in action, as the consummation of all good.   (17-437)

(19)   . . . death is just a method for refocussing energy, prior to a forward moving activity, leading steadily and always towards betterment.   (17-297)

(20)   . . . for a free soul, death and the taking of a form and the consequent immersion of the life in the form, are synonymous terms.   (17-439)

(21)   The fear and the morbidness which the subject of death usually evokes, and the unwillingness to face it with understanding are due to the emphasis which people lay upon the fact of the physical body and the facility with which they identify themselves with it; it is based also upon an innate fear of loneliness and the loss of the familiar. Yet the loneliness which eventuates after death, when the man finds himself without a physical vehicle, is as nothing compared to the loneliness of birth. At birth, the soul finds itself in new surroundings and immersed in a body which is at first totally incompetent to take care of itself or to establish intelligent contact with surrounding conditions for a long period of time. The man comes into incarnation with no recollection as to the identity or the significance to him of the group of souls in bodies with which he finds himself in relationship; this loneliness only disappears gradually as he makes his own personality contacts, discovers those who are congenial to him and eventually gathers around him those whom he calls his friends. After death this is not so, for the man finds on the other side of the veil those whom he knows and who have been connected with him in physical plane life, and he is never alone as human beings understand loneliness; he is also conscious of those still in physical bodies; he can see them, he can tune in on their emotions, and also upon their thinking, for the physical brain, being nonexistent, no longer acts as a deterrent. If people but knew more, birth would be the experience which they

would dread, and not death, for birth establishes the soul in the true prison, and physical death is only the first step towards liberation.   (17-392/3)

PART IX

Death comes to the individual man, in the ordinary sense of the term, when the will-to-live in a physical body goes and the will-to-abstract takes its place. This we call death.

(18-164/5)

PART IX

(1)   WHEN THE cause, desire, has produced its effect, the personality or form aspect of man, then as long as the will to live exists, so long will the form persist. It is kept in manifestation through mental vitality. This has been demonstrated time and again in the annals of medicine, for it has been proven that as long as the determination to live persists, so will be the probable duration of the physical plane life; but that the moment that will is withdrawn, or the interest of the dweller in the body is no longer centered upon personality manifestation, death ensues and the disintegration of that mind-image, the body, takes place.   (17-452/3)

(2)   Intense desire for sentient existence or attachment . . . is inherent in every form, is self-perpetuating and known even to the very wise.

When the life or spirit withdraws itself, the form dies, occultly. When the thought of the ego* or higher self is occupied with its own plane, there is no energy outgoing towards the matter of the three worlds, and so no form-building and form-attachment is there possible. This is in line with the occult truism that "energy follows thought," and is in line, too, with the teaching that the body of the Christ principle (the Buddhic vehicle) only begins to coordinate as the lower impulses fade out . . . . Attachment to form or the attraction of form for Spirit is the great involutionary impulse. Repulsion of form and consequent form disintegration is the great evolutionary urge.   (17-452)

(3)   Death, when it comes, is the result of two things:

1. The fight between the forces, and not between energy and the forces. The area of conflict is the etheric body and the physical body, and no energies are coming in from without because the man is too ill.

---

*ego, or soul (see glossary).

2. The loss of the will-to-live. The patient has given in; the internal fight is too much for him; he can bring in no outside energy to combat the warring forces, and he has reached the point where he does not want to do so.   (17-596)

(4)   It will be obvious to you that this Principle of Conflict is closely related to death. By death, I mean extraction from form conditions—physical, emotional or mental; I mean cessation of contact (temporarily or permanently) with physical form, with astral glamour and with mental illusion; I mean the rejection of Maya, the name of that all-inclusive effect which overwhelms a man who is immersed in materialism of any kind, and is therefore overcome (from the soul angle) by life in the three worlds. It is the Principle of Conflict, latent in every atom of substance, which produces, first of all, conflict, then renunciation, and finally emancipation; which produces war in some form or another, then rejection, and finally liberation. This principle is, as you can well see, closely linked to the law of Karma; it is to this principle that Mrs. Besant refers when she speaks in one of her books of the fact that the substance whereof all forms are made is already—from the very dawn of the creative process—tinged with karma. There is deep occult significance to the thought, often voiced, that death is the great Liberator; it means that the Principle of Conflict has succeeded in bringing about conditions wherein the spirit aspect is released (temporarily or permanently) from imprisonment in some kind of form life, either individual or group.   (18-607)

(5)   It is interesting to note that this inability to express "the true" or to "be the Truth" is the real cause of death among men who are below the stage of discipleship and who have not yet taken the first initiation. The soul tires of the frictional response of its instrument and determines to end the experiment of that particular incarnation. Death, therefore, supervenes as a result of the friction engendered.   (17-568)

(6)   It must be noted also that death is, therefore, undertaken at the direction of the ego, no matter how unaware a human being may be of that direction. The process works automatically with the majority, for when the soul withdraws its attention the inevitable reaction on the physical plane is death, either by the abstraction of the dual threads of life and reason energy, or by the abstraction of the thread of energy which is qualified by mentality, leaving the life stream still functioning through the heart but no

intelligent awareness. The soul is engaged elsewhere and occupied on its own plane with its own affairs.   (4-497/8)

(7)   The intent is for men to die, as every man has to die, *at the demand of his own soul.* When man has reached a higher stage in evolution, with deliberation and definite choice of time, he will consciously withdraw from his physical body. It will be left silent and empty of the soul; devoid of light, yet sound and whole; it will then disintegrate, under the natural process, and its constituent atoms will pass back into "the pool of waiting units," until they are again required for the use of incarnating souls. Again, on the subjective side of life, the process is repeated, but many have already learnt to withdraw from the astral body without being subject to that "impact in the fog," which is the symbolic way of describing the death of a man upon the astral plane. He then withdraws on to the mental level, and leaves his astral carcass to swell the fog and increase its density.   (17-29)

(8)   Death, as far as the human being is concerned, is increasingly due to the *planned* intent and *planned* withdrawal of the soul, under the pressure of its own formulated intent. This is true to some degree of all who die, except those who are of so low a grade of intelligence that the soul is practically little more than an overshadowing agency. Of all who die, highly developed or not, the later stages of dissolution, effective after the conscious withdrawal of the soul (conscious on the part of the soul and becoming increasingly conscious on the part of the dying person), are taken over by this death-bestowing power of the planetary life itself.   (17-244)

(9)   *By the development of goodwill,* which is the will of good intention and motive, will come the healing of diseases of the respiratory tract, lungs and throat, the stablising of cells of the brain, the cure of insanities and obsessions, and an attainment of equilibrium and of rhythm. Longevity will ensue, for death should be the recognition by the soul of work consummated and pralaya earned. It will only take place later at long and separated periods, and will be controlled by the will of the man. He will cease to breathe when he has finished his work, and then will send the atoms of his body into pralaya. That is the sleep of the physical, the end of manifestation, and the occult significance of this is not yet comprehended.   (17-108)

(10)   I would ask you to remember that in all our present

considerations we are dealing with the reactions and activities of the soul which is deliberately recalling its incarnated aspect because a life cycle has been concluded. The term of that life cycle may be long or short, according to the purposes involved; it may cover only a very few short years, or a century. Prior to the seventh year, the vitality of the physical elemental is largely the determining factor. The soul is then focussed in the etheric body, but is not fully utilizing all the centres; it has simply a gently pulsating control and a gentle impulsive activity — sufficient to preserve consciousness, to vitalise the various physical processes, and to initiate the demonstration of character and of disposition. These become increasingly marked until the twenty-first year, when they stabilise into what we call the personality. In the case of disciples, the grip of the soul upon the etheric centres will be more powerful from the very start of the physical existence. By the time the fourteenth year is reached, the quality and the nature of the incarnated soul and its approximate age or experience are determined, the physical, astral and mental elementals are under control, and the soul, the indwelling spiritual man, already determines the life tendencies and choice.   (17-463/4)

(11)   In the human family, death supervenes when the soul withdraws its consciousness thread and its life thread; this process of death is contained, however, entirely within the three worlds. The soul has its station on the higher levels of the mental plane, as well you know. In connection with the forms of expression to which I have referred above — cycles, civilisations, cultures, races, kingdoms in nature and so forth — their destruction is brought about from still higher sources than the three worlds in which they manifest. This destruction takes place under the direction of Shamballa as it evokes the will of the Hierarchy or some particular Ashram or some member of the Hierarchy in order to produce a predetermined result in the three worlds in line with the purpose of God. It might be said (accurately to a certain esoteric extent) that the destruction brought about in obedience to this fourth word in Rule XIV is the destruction of some aspect of the plan as it has been functioning in the three worlds, and this under divine purpose and intent.

          This destruction is not outwardly so conclusive as is death — on the physical plane — of a man, though that is not essentially the rapidly consummated process as is usually surmised. The physical form may die and disappear, but an inner process of dying of the subtler bodies supervenes and the death process is not complete until the astral and mental bodies have disintegrated and the man stands free in his causal or soul body. So it is, on a much larger scale, with the death or destruction of phases of the divine Plan, engineered by the Hierarchy in conformity with the divine Purpose. There is an overlapping between the building process and the destroying process. Dying civilisations are present in their final forms whilst new civilisations are emerging; cycles come and go and in the going overlap; the same is also found to be true in the emerging and disappearing of rays and races. Death, in the last analysis and from the standpoint of the average human being, is simply disappearance from the physical plane—the plane of appearances.   (18-308/9)

PART X

As humanity becomes soul-conscious . . . death will be seen as an "ordered" process, carried out in full consciousness and with understanding of cyclic purpose.   (17-435/6)

PART X

(1) $\quad$ I DEALT with the subject of death in *A Treatise on White Magic,* focussing therein primarily upon the physical processes of dying and doing so from the point of view of the onlooker or observer. I sought there to indicate what the attitude of the onlooker should be. Here I would like to present a somewhat different picture, indicating what is known by the departing soul. If this involves repetition of what you already know, there are however certain basic repetitions and statements I wish to make. Let me tabulate them with brevity. Will you regard them as foundational and factual.

1. The time for the departure of an incarnating soul has come. The soul has in the past:
   a. Appropriated a physical body of a certain calibre, adequate to the requirements and age of that soul.
   b. Energised that physical body through the medium of the etheric body, thus galvanising it into life activity for the duration of the soul's set term of physical enterprise.
2. Two major streams of energy enter the physical body and produce its activity, its quality and type of expression, plus the impression it makes upon its environment.
   a. *The stream of dynamic life.* This is anchored in the heart. This stream of dynamic energy enters the body, via the head, and passes down to the heart, where it is focussed during the life cycle. A smaller stream of the universal energy or prana, distinctive from the individualised life force, enters the physical body, via the spleen. It then rises to the heart to join the larger and more important life stream. The life stream energises and holds in coherency the integrated physical body. The stream of pranic energy vitalises the individual atoms and cells of which that body is composed.
   b. *The stream of individual consciousness.* This is anchored in the head, is an aspect of the soul, reveals the type of consciousness which is, in its turn, indicative of the point attained

in evolution. This stream of energy likewise functions in connection with a stream of personality force; and this force is characterised by desire (emotional or astral sentiency) and enters into the physical body, via the solar plexus centre. This relates the man to the entire astral plane, and therefore to the world of glamour. With undeveloped people and with the average type of man, the solar plexus is the focus of consciousness and the energy is registered by the focal point of consciousness in the head without any recognition whatsoever. It is for this reason that (at the time of death) the soul leaves the body, via the solar plexus and not via the head. In the case of the developed man, the mental type of individual, the aspirant, disciple or initiate, the thread of consciousness will withdraw from the body via the head.

3. The group soul of all forms in the animal kingdom—under the Law of Attraction—withdraws the life principle from any specific physical form via the solar plexus, which is the brain of the average animal. Highly developed and domesticated animals are beginning to utilise the brain to a greater or to a less degree, but the life principle and the sentient aspect, or animal consciousness, is still withdrawn via the solar plexus. You have, therefore, in all stages of the evolutionary process, certain interesting triangles of energy.

a. In the case of the animals and of those human beings who are little more than animals, of imbeciles and certain men who appear to be born with no centralised point of individual consciousness, the following triplicity is of importance:

    The group soul

    The solar plexus

    The spleen or pranic centre.

b. In low grade, but nevertheless individualised human beings and with the average emotional type of person, the following triplicity must be noted:

    The soul

    The head centre

    The solar plexus.

c. For highly developed people and for those upon the Path of Discipleship you have the following triangle active at the time of death:

    The soul

The head centre

The ajna centre.

In connection with all these triplicities there exists a dual relationship to the life principle:

a. The heart in which is focussed the life of the soul in form.

b. The spleen through which passes constantly and rhythmically the universal life essence or prana.

The whole subject is of course most obscure, and for those on strictly human levels, as yet unverifiable. However, an acceptance of the above three points, hypothetical today, will help to clarify your minds concerning this entire theme of restitution with which we are occupied.

4. The next point needs no proving, for it is generally accepted. It is that desire governs the process of death, as it also governs the processes of life experience. We say constantly that when the will-to-live is lacking, death is the inevitable result. This will-to-live, whether it is the tenacity of the physical body, functioning as an elemental being or as the directed intention of the soul, is an aspect of desire, or rather, it is a reaction of the spiritual will upon the physical plane. There is therefore an interlocking relation between:

a. The soul on its own plane.

b. The astral body.

c. The solar plexus centre.

This relationship has hitherto received little attention in connection with the Art of Dying. Nevertheless it warrants careful thought.   (17-428/31)

(2)   The process of DEATH is occultly as follows:

a. The first stage is the withdrawal of the life force in the etheric vehicle from the dense physical body and the consequent "falling into corruption" and becoming "scattered to the elements." Objective man fades out and is no more seen by the physical eye, though still in his etheric body. When etheric vision is developed, the thought of death will assume very different proportions. When a man can be seen functioning in his etheric physical body by a majority of the race, the dropping of the dense body will be considered just as a release.

b. The second stage is the withdrawal of the life force from the etheric body, and its devitalisation. . . .

c. The third stage is the withdrawal of the life force from the astral or emotional form so that it disintegrates in a similar manner and the life is centralised elsewhere. It has gained an increase of vitality through physical plane existence and added colour through emotional experience.

d. The final stage for the human being is its withdrawal from the mental vehicle. The life forces after this fourfold abstraction are centralised entirely in the soul. . . .   (17-414/5)

(3)   I feel that the best that I can do, in order to clarify this subject more completely, is to describe the sequence of events which happens at a death bed, reminding you that the points of final abstraction are three in number: the head for disciples and initiates and also for advanced mental types; the heart for aspirants, for men of goodwill, and for all those who have achieved a measure of personality integrity and are attempting to fulfill, as far as in them lies, the law of love; and the solar plexus for the undeveloped and emotionally polarised persons. All I can do is to tabulate the stages of the process, leaving you to accept them as an interesting and possible hypothesis awaiting verification; to believe them unquestioningly because you have confidence in my knowledge, or to reject them as fantastic, unverifiable and of no moment anyway. I recommend the first of the three, for it will enable you to preserve your mental integrity, it will indicate an open mind, and at the same time it will protect you from gullibility and from narrow-mindedness. These stages, therefore, are:

1. *The soul sounds forth a "word of withdrawal"* from its own plane, and immediately an interior process and reaction is evoked within the man upon the physical plane.
    a. *Certain physiological events* take place at the seat of the disease, in connection with the heart, and affecting also the three great systems which so potently condition the physical man: the blood stream, the nervous system in its various expressions, and the endocrine system. With these effects I shall not deal. The pathology of death is well known and has received much study exoterically; much still remains to be discovered and will later be discovered. I am concerned, first of all, with the subjective reactions which (in the last analysis) bring about the pathological predisposition to death.
    b. *A vibration runs along the nadis.* The nadis are, as you well know, the etheric counterpart of the entire nervous system,

and they underlie every single nerve in the entire physical body. They are the agents par excellence of the directing impulses of the soul, reacting to the vibratory activity which emanates from the etheric counterpart of the brain. They respond to the directing Word, react to the "pull" of the soul, and then organise themselves for abstraction.

c. *The blood stream becomes affected* in a peculiarly occult manner. The "blood is the life," we are told, it is interiorly changed as a result of the two previous stages, but primarily as the result of an activity hitherto undiscovered by modern science, for which the glandular system is responsible. The glands, in response to the call of death, inject into the blood stream a substance which in turn affects the heart. There the life thread is anchored, and this substance in the blood is regarded as "death-dealing" and is one of the basic causes of coma and of loss of consciousness. It evokes a reflex action in the brain. This substance and its effect will be questioned as yet by orthodox medicine, but its presence will later be recognized.

d. *A psychic tremor is established* which has the effect of loosening or breaking the connection between the nadis and the nervous system; the etheric body is thereby detached from its dense sheath, though still interpenetrating every part of it.

2. *There is frequently a pause* at this point of a shorter or longer period of time. This is allowed in order to carry forward the loosening process as smoothly and as painlessly as possible. This loosening of the nadis starts in the eyes. This process of detachment often shows itself in the relaxation and lack of fear which dying persons so often show; they evidence a condition of peace, and a willingness to go, plus an inability to make a mental effort. It is as if the dying person, still preserving his consciousness, gathers his resources together for the final abstraction. This is the stage in which—the fear of death once and for all removed from the racial mind—the friends and relatives of the departing person will "make a festival" for him and will rejoice with him because he is relinquishing the body. At present this is not possible. Distress rules, and the stage passes unrecognised and is not utilised, as it will some day be.

3. *Next, the organised etheric body,* loosened from all nervous relationship through the action of the nadis, *begins to gather itself*

together for the final departure. It withdraws from the extremities towards the required "door of exit" and focusses itself in the area around that door for the final "pull" of the directing soul. All has been proceeding under the Law of Attraction up to this point—the magnetic, attractive will of the soul. Now another "pull" or attractive impulse makes itself felt. The dense physical body, the sumtotal of organs, cells and atoms, is steadily being released from the integrating potency of the vital body by the action of the nadis; it begins to respond to the attractive pull of matter itself. This has been called the "earth" pull and is exerted by that mysterious entity whom we call the "spirit of the earth"; this entity is on the involutionary arc, and is to our planet what the physical elemental is to the physical body of man. This physical plane life force is essentially the life and light of atomic substance—the matter of which all forms are made. It is to this reservoir of involutionary and material life that the substance of all forms is restored. Restitution of the commandeered matter of the form occupied by the soul during a life cycle consists in returning to this "Caesar" of the involutionary world what is his, whilst the soul returns to the God Who sent it forth.

It will therefore be apparent that a dual attractive process is at this stage going on:

a. The vital body is being prepared for exit.

b. The physical body is responding to dissolution.

It might be added that a third activity is also present. It is that of the conscious man, withdrawing his consciousness, steadily and gradually, into the astral and mental vehicles, preparatory to the complete abstraction of the etheric body when the right time comes. The man is becoming less and less attached to the physical plane and more withdrawn within himself. In the case of an advanced person, this process is consciously undertaken, and the man retains his vital interests and his awareness of relationship to others even whilst losing his grip on physical existence. In old age this detachment can be more easily noted than in death through disease, and frequently the soul or the living, interested, inner man can be seen losing his grip on physical and, therefore illusory reality.

4. *Again a pause ensues.* This is the point where the physical elemental can at times regain its hold upon the etheric body, if that is deemed desirable by the soul, if death is not part of the

inner plan, or if the physical elemental is so powerful that it can prolong the process of dying. This elemental life will sometimes fight a battle lasting for days and weeks. When, however, death is inevitable, the pause at this point will be exceedingly brief, sometimes only for a matter of seconds. The physical elemental has lost its hold, and the etheric body awaits the final "tug" from the soul, acting under the Law of Attraction.

5. *The etheric body emerges from the dense physical body* in gradual stages and at the chosen point of exit. When this emergence is complete, the vital body then assumes the vague outline of the form that it energised, and this under the influence of the thoughtform of himself which the man has built up over the years. This thoughtform exists in the case of every human being, and must be destroyed before the second stage of elimination is finally complete. We will touch upon this later. Though freed from the prison of the physical body, the etheric body is not yet freed from its influence. There is still a slight rapport between the two, and this keeps the spiritual man still close to the body just vacated. That is why clairvoyants often claim to see the etheric body hovering around the death bed or the coffin. Still interpenetrating the etheric body are the integrated energies which we call the astral body and the mental vehicle, and at the centre there is a point of light which indicates the presence of the soul.

6. *The etheric body is gradually dispersed* as the energies of which it is composed are reorganised and withdrawn, leaving only the pranic substance which is identified with the etheric vehicle of the planet itself. This process of dispersal is, as I have earlier said, greatly aided by cremation. In the case of the undeveloped person, the etheric body can linger for a long time in the neighbourhood of its outer disintegrating shell because the pull of the soul is not potent and the material aspect is. Where the person is advanced, and therefore detached in his thinking from the physical plane, the dissolution of the vital body can be exceedingly rapid. Once it is accomplished, the process of restitution is over; the man is freed, temporarily at least, from all reaction to the attractive pull of physical matter; he stands in his subtle bodies, ready for the great act to which I have given the name "The Art of Elimination."

One thought emerges as we conclude this inadequate consideration of the death of the physical body in its two aspects: that thought is the integrity of the inner man. *He remains himself.* He is untouched and untrammelled; he is a free agent as far as the physical plane is concerned, and is responsive now to only three predisposing factors:

1. The quality of his astral-emotional equipment.
2. The mental condition in which he habitually lives.
3. The voice of the soul, often unfamiliar but sometimes well known and loved.

Individuality is not lost; the same person is still present upon the planet. Only that has disappeared which was an integral part of the tangible appearance of our planet. That which has been loved or hated, which has been useful to humanity or a liability, which has served the race or been an ineffectual member of it, still persists, is still in touch with the qualitative and mental processes of existence, and will forever remain—individual, qualified by ray type, part of the kingdom of souls, and a high initiate in his own right.   (17-472/8)

(4)   Before I take up this subject in greater detail I would like to make reference to the "web in the brain", which is intact for the majority but is non-existent for the illumined seer.

In the human body, as you know, we have an underlying, interpenetrating vital body which is the counterpart of the physical, which is larger than the physical and which we call the etheric body or double. It is an energy body and is composed of force centres and nadis or force threads. These underlie or are the counterparts of the nervous apparatus—the nerves and the nerve ganglia. In two places in the human vital body there are *orifices of exit* for the life force. One opening is in the solar plexus and the other is in the brain at the top of the head. Protecting both is a closely woven web of etheric matter, composed of interlacing strands of life energy.

During the process of death, the pressure of the life energy beating against the web produces eventually a puncturing or opening. Out of this the life force pours as the potency of the abstracting influence of the soul increases. In the case of animals, of infants and of men and women who are polarized entirely in the physical and astral bodies, the door of exit is the solar plexus and it is that web which is punctured, thus permitting the passing out. In the case of mental types, of the more highly evolved human units, it is the web at the top of the head in the region of the fontanelle which is ruptured, thus again permitting the exit of the thinking rational being.

In psychics and in the case of mediums and lower seers (clairvoyant and clairaudient people) the solar plexus web is permanently ruptured early in life and easily therefore they pass in or out of the body, going into trance, as it is called, and functioning on the astral plane. But for these types there is no continuity of consciousness and there seems no relation between their physical plane existence and the happenings which they relate whilst in trance and of which they usually remain totally unaware in the waking consciousness. The whole performance is below the diaphragm and is related primarily to animal sentient life. In the case of conscious clairvoyance and in the work of the higher psychics and seers there is no trance, obsession or mediumship. It is the web in the brain which is punctured and the opening in that region permits the inflow of light, information and inspiration; it confers also the power to pass into the state of Samadhi which is the spiritual correspondence to the trance condition of the animal nature.

In the process of death these are, therefore, the two main exits: the solar plexus for the astrally polarized, physically biased human being and therefore of the vast majority, and the head centre for the mentally polarized and spiritually oriented human being. This is the first and most important fact to remember and it will easily be seen how the trend of a life tendency and the focus of the life attention determine the mode of exit at death. It can be seen also that an effort to control the astral life and the emotional nature and to orient one's self to the mental world and to spiritual things has a momentous effect upon the phenomenal aspects of the death process.

If the student is thinking clearly, it will be apparent to him that one exit concerns the spiritual and highly evolved man, whilst the other concerns the low grade human being who scarcely advanced beyond the animal stage. What then of the averge man? A third exit is now in temporary use; just below the apex of the heart another etheric web is found covering an orifice of exit. We have, therefore, the following situation:

1. The exit in the head, used by the intellectual type, by the disciples and initiates of the world.

2. The exit in the heart, used by the kindly, well-meaning man or woman who is a good citizen, an intelligent friend and a philanthropic worker.
3. The exit in the region of the solar plexus, used by the emotional, unintelligent, unthinking man and by those whose animal nature is strong.

This is the first point in the new information which will slowly become common knowledge in the West during the next century. Much of it is already known by thinkers in the East and is in the nature of the first step towards a rational understanding of the death process.   (4/500/2)

(5)   I have sought, in the preceding pages, to give an insight into the true nature of that which we call death. Death is the withdrawal, consciously or unconsciously, of the inner living entity from its outer shell, its inner vital correspondence, and finally it is the relinquishing of the subtle body or bodies, according to the point in evolution of the person. I have also sought to show the normality of this familiar process. The horror which attends death upon the battlefield or by accident consists in the shock which it precipitates within the area of the etheric body, necessitating a rapid rearrangement of its constituent forces and a sudden and unexpected reintegration of its component parts in response to definite action which has perforce to be taken by the man in his kama-manasic body. This action does not involve the replacing of the inner man again within the etheric vehicle, but requires a coming together of the dissipated aspects of that body under the Law of Attraction, in order that its final and complete dissolution can take place.   (17-478/9)

(6)   Again, the death process can be seen as a dual activity and one which primarily concerns the etheric body. There is first of all the collecting and the withdrawing of the etheric substance, so that it no longer interpenetrates the dense physical organism, and its subsequent *densification* (a word I deliberately choose) in that area of the etheric body which has always surrounded, but not penetrated, the dense vehicle. This has been sometimes erroneously called the health aura, and it can be photographed more easily and successfully during the process of dying than at any other time, owing to the accumulation of the withdrawn forces for several inches external to the tangible body. It is at this point in the experience of the withdrawing soul that the "word of death" is spoken, and it is prior to this enunciation of this word that a return

to physical living can be possible and the withdrawn etheric forces can again interpenetrate the body. Relationship with all the withdrawn forces is, up to this point, retained via the head or the heart or the solar plexus, as well as via the two minor chest centres.

All this time the consciousness of the dying man is focussed in either the emotional (or astral) body or the mental vehicle, according to the point in evolution. He is not unconscious as the onlooker might infer, but is fully aware within himself of what is occurring. If he is strongly focussed on physical plane life, and if that is the dominating desire of which he is the most aware, he may then intensify the conflict; you will then have the physical elemental battling furiously for existence, the desire nature fighting to retard the processes of death, and the soul, intent upon the work of abstraction and of restitution. This can and frequently does occasion a struggle which is quite apparent to the onlookers. As the race of men progresses and develops, this triple struggle will become much rarer; desire for physical plane existence will not appear so attractive, and the activity of the astral body will die out.   (17-466/7)

(7)   There is a great abstracting energy which we call Death, whose influence at a given time proves more potent than the united influences of the body atoms and cells. It produces the tendency to withdraw and finally to abstract the soul energy which avails itself of these potencies in the process of discarding a vehicle on some plane or another. It might be said that the seeds of death (the germ of death) are latent in the planet and in the forms.   (17-347)

(8)   It is the centres which hold the body together and make it a coherent, energised and active whole. As you know, when death takes place, the consciousness thread withdraws from the head centre and the life thread withdraws from the heart centre. What has not been emphasised is that this dual withdrawal has an effect upon every centre in the body. The consciousness thread, anchored in the head centre, qualifies the petals of the lotus called in the oriental literature the "thousand-petalled lotus," and the petals of that lotus have a relationship and a definitely qualifying effect (both radiatory and magnetic) upon the petals in every one of the other major centres within the etheric body; the head centre preserves them in qualifying activity, and when this quality of conscious response is withdrawn from the head centre an immediate effect is felt in all the petals of all the centres; the qualifying

energy is withdrawn, leaving the body via the head centre. The same general technique is true of the life thread which is anchored in the heart, after passing (in alliance with the consciousness thread) into and through the head centre. As long as the life thread is anchored in the heart it energises and preserves in living-ness all the centres in the body, sending out its threads of life into a point which is found at the exact centre of the lotus, or at the heart of the centre. This is sometimes called "the jewel in the lotus," though the phrase is more frequently applied to the monadic point at the heart of the egoic lotus on its own plane. When death takes place and the life thread is gathered up by the soul and withdrawn from the heart into the head and from thence back into the soul body, it carries with it the life of each centre in the body; therefore, the body dies and disintegrates, and no longer forms a coherent, conscious, living whole.   (17-622/3)

(9)   The etheric forces are first of all withdrawn into the surrounding extension of the etheric ring-pass-not, prior to that final dissipation which leaves the man free to stand as a human soul within the ring-pass-not of his astral vehicle. You have here a somewhat new aspect of the death process. The withdrawal of the etheric body from occupation of the dense physical body has oft been posited and presented. But even when that has been accomplished, death is not yet complete; it still awaits a secondary activity of the will of the soul. This secondary activity will result in all the etheric forces dissolving into an emanating source which is the general reservoir of forces. Forget not that the etheric body has no distinctive life of its own. It is only an amalgamation of all the forces and energies which animated the physical body and which galvanised it into activity during the outer life cycle. Remember also that the five centres up the spine are not within the physical body, but are found at certain distinctive points in the paralleling etheric substance; they are (even in the case of the undeveloped man, and still more in the case of the average man) at least two inches away from the physical spine. The three head centres are also outside the dense physical body. The recollection of this will facilitate your understanding of the statement that the physical body is, *per se,* vacated when death is assumed by the watching authorities, but that, nevertheless, the man may not be truly dead. I would remind you also that this is equally true of the many minor centres as well as of the major centres, with which we are so familiar.

The last of the minor centres to "fade out into nothingness," in order to be resolved into the totality of etheric substance, are two which are closely related to and in the region of the lungs. It is on these two centres that the soul works if recalled into the dense physical body for some reason. It is when they swing into a returning or a fresh in-going activity that the breath of life returns to the vacated physical form. It is an unconscious realisation of this which constitutes the prompting cause of the process which is normally carried out in all cases of drowning or of asphyxiation. When a man has succumbed to disease and the physical body is consequently weakened, such restorative exercises are not possible and should not be employed. In cases of sudden death through accident, suicide, murder, unexpected heart attacks or through the processes of war, the shock is such that the somewhat leisurely process of soul withdrawal is entirely offset, and the vacating of the physical body and the complete dissolution of the etheric body are practically simultaneous. In normal cases of death from disease, the withdrawal is slow, and (where the malignancy of the disease has not caused too great deterioration of the physical organism involved) there is the possibility of a return for a shorter or a longer period of time. This frequently happens, especially when the will to live is strong or the life task remains as yet unaccomplished and is not correctly concluded.   (17-460/2)

(10)   The changes wrought in the centres when the death of the physical body is taking place have never yet been observed or recorded; they are, however, definitely present to the eye of the initiate and prove most interesting and informative. It is the recognition of the condition of the centres which enables the initiate to know — when in process of bestowing healing — whether the physical healing of the body is permissible or not. He can see whether the will principle of abstraction to which I have been referring is actively present or not. The same process can be seen taking place in organisations and in civilisations in which the form aspect is being destroyed in order that life may be abstracted and later again rebuild for itself a more adequate form. It is the same under the great processes of initiation, which are not only processes of expanding the consciousness but are rooted in the death or the abstraction process, leading to resurrection and ascension.

That which effects a change is a *discharge* (to use a totally inadequate phrase) of directed and focussed will-energy. This is so magnetic in quality that it draws to itself the life of the centres, bringing about the dissolution of the form and the release of the life. Death comes to the individual man, in the ordinary sense of the term, when the will-to-live in a physical body goes and the will-to-abstract takes its place. This we call death. In cases of death in war, for instance, it is not then a case of the individual will-to-withdraw, but an enforced participation in a great group abstraction. From its own place, the soul of the individual man recognizes the end of a cycle of incarnation and recalls its life. This it does through a discharge of the will-energy that is strong enough to bring about the change.

2. *The Law demands that right direction should then guide the entering forces.*

The entering forces, working under this law, are directed first of all to the head centre, from thence to the ajna centre and then to that centre which has been the governing and most active centre during the incarnation of the life principle. This varies according to the point reached upon the ladder of evolution, and according to the personality ray, with later the soul ray bringing about a major conditioning and change. In the work of the initiate who is consciously wielding this law, the principle of abstraction (when entering the body) is held focussed in the head and is of such a magnetic potency that the energy of the remaining centres is rapidly gathered up and withdrawn. What is true of the individual process of abstracting the life principle, under the Law of Supplementary Seven, is equally true of the process in all forms and in all groups of forms. Christ referred to this work of abstraction, as regards the third great planetary centre, Humanity, when He said (and He was speaking as the Representative of the Hierarchy, the second planetary centre into which all human beings achieving initiation are "withdrawn" esoterically), "I, if I be lifted up will draw all men unto me." A different word to this word of His will be spoken at the end of the age when the Lord of the World will speak from Shamballa, will abstract the life principle from the Hierarchy, and all life and consciousness will then be focussed in the planetary head centre—the great Council Chamber at Shamballa.   (18-164/5)

(11)   To take up again the thread of our instruction, we will now consider the activity of the inner spiritual man who has discarded his physical and etheric bodies and now stands within the shell of the subtle body—a body composed of astral or sentient

substance and of mental substance. Owing to the strongly emotional and sentient polarisation of the average man, the idea has taken hold that man withdraws, after true death, first of all into his astral body, and then, later, into his mental vehicle. But this is not actually the case. A body constructed predominantly of astral matter is the basis of this idea. Few people are as yet so developed that the vehicle in which they find themselves after death is largely composed of mental substance. Only disciples and initiates who live mostly in their minds find themselves, after death, immediately upon the mental plane. Most people discover themselves upon the astral plane, clothed in a shell of astral matter and committed to a period of elimination within the illusory area of the astral plane.

As I have earlier told you, the astral plane has no factual existence, but is an illusory creation of the human family. From now on, however (through the defeat of the forces of evil and the disastrous setback suffered by the Black Lodge), the astral plane will slowly become a dying creation, and in the final period of human history (in the seventh rootrace), it will become nonexistent. Today this is not the case. The sentient substance which constitutes the astral plane is still being gathered into forms of illusion and still forms a barrier in the path of the soul seeking liberation. It still "holds prisoner" the many people who die whilst their major reaction to life is that of desire, of wishful thinking and of emotional sentiency. These are still the vast majority. In Atlantean days the astral plane came into being; the mental state of consciousness was then practically non-existent, though the "sons of mind" had their place on what is today the higher levels of that plane. The mental permanent atom was also practically quiescent within each human form, and there was consequently no attractive "pull" from the mental plane, as is the case today. Many people are still Atlantean in consciousness, and when they pass out of the physical state of consciousness and discard their dual physical body, they are faced with the problem of elimination of the astral body, but they have little to do to release themselves from any mental prison of the soul. These are the undeveloped and average persons who, after the elimination of the kamic or desire body, have little else to do; there is no mental vehicle to draw them into a mental integration because there is no mentally focussed potency; the soul on the higher mental levels is as yet "in deep meditation" and quite unaware of its shadow in the three worlds.   (17-486/7)

(1) THE FIELD of experience (in which is death, as the average person knows it) is the three worlds of human evolution — the physical world, the world of emotion and desire, and the mental plane. This world is, in the last analysis two-fold, from the angle of death, and hence the phrase "the second death." This I have earlier applied to the death or destruction of the causal body, in which the spiritual soul has hitherto functioned. It can be applied, however, in a more literal sense, and may be referred to the second phase of the death process in the three worlds. It then concerns form only, and is related to those vehicles of expression which are found below the formless levels of the cosmic physical plane. These form levels are (as you know well, for the knowledge constitutes the a.b.c. of the occult theory) the levels on which the concrete, lower mind functions, the emotional nature reacts to the so-called astral plane, and the dual physical plane. The physical body consists of the dense physical body and the etheric vehicle. We have consequently, when considering the death of a human being, to employ the word death in relation to two phases in which it functions:

Phase One: The death of the physical-etheric body. This phase falls into two stages:

a. That in which the atoms which constitute the physical body are restored to the source from whence they came. This source is the sumtotal of the matter of the planet, constituting the dense physical body of the planetary Life.
b. That in which the etheric vehicle, composed of an aggregation of forces, returns these forces to the general reservoir of energy. *This dual phase covers the Process of Restitution.*

Phase Two: The "rejection" (as it is sometimes called) of the mental-emotional vehicles. These form, in reality, only one body; to it the early theosophists (correctly) gave the name of the "kama-manasic body" or the vehicle of desire-mind. I have said elsewhere that there is no such thing as the astral plane or the astral body. Just as the physical body is made up of matter which is not regarded as a principle, so the astral body — as far as the mind nature is concerned — is in the same category. This is a difficult matter for you to grasp, because desire and emotion are so real and so devastatingly important. But — speaking literally — from the angle of the mental plane, the astral body is "a figment of the imagination"; it is *not* a principle. The massed use of ·the imagination in the service of desire has nevertheless constructed an illusory glamorous world, the world of the astral plane. During physical incarnation, and when a man is not upon the Path of Discipleship, the astral plane is very real, with a vitality and a life all its own. After the first death (the death of the physical body) it still remains equally real. But its potency slowly dies out; the mental man comes to realise his own true state of consciousness (whether developed or undeveloped), and the second death becomes possible and takes place. *This phase covers the Process of Elimination.*

When these two phases of the Art of Dying are over, the discarnate soul stands free from the control of matter; it is purified (temporarily by the phases of Restitution and Elimination) from all contamination by substance. This is achieved, not through any activity of the soul in form, the human soul, but as a result of the activity of the soul on its own plane abstracting the fraction of itself which we call the human soul. It is primarily the work of the overshadowing soul which effects this; it is not carried forward by the soul in the personality. The human soul, during this stage, is only responsive to the pull or the attractive force of the spiritual soul as it — with deliberate intent — extracts the human soul from its imprisoning sheaths. Later on, as the evolutionary processes proceed and the soul increasingly controls the personality, it will bring about — consciously and with intention — the phases of dying. In the earlier stages, this release will be brought about with the aid of the overshadowing spiritual soul. Later on, when the man is living upon the physical plane as the soul, he will himself — with full continuity of consciousness — carry out the processes of abstraction, and will then (with directed purpose) "ascend to the place from whence he came." This is the reflection in the three worlds of the divine ascension of the perfected Son of God.   (17-408/10)

(2)   You will note that the various words I have chosen in considering the basic requirements have been so chosen for their specific meanings:

1. *The Work of Restitution* signifies the returning of the form to the basic reservoir of substance; or of the soul, the divine spiritual energy, returning to its source—either on soul or monadic levels, accordings to the point in evolution. This restitution is predominantly the work of the human soul within the physical body and involves both the heart and the head centres.

2. *The Art of Elimination.* This refers to two activities of the inner spiritual man; i.e., the elimination of all control by the threefold lower man, and the process of refocussing itself upon the concrete levels of the mental plane as a point of radiant light. This concerns primarily the human soul.

3. *The Processes of Integration.* These deal with the work of the liberated spiritual man as he blends with the soul (the oversoul) upon the higher levels of the mental plane. The part returns to the whole, and the man comprehends the true meaning of the words of Krishna, "Having pervaded this whole universe with a fragment of myself, I remain." He, too, the conscious experiencing fragment which has pervaded the little universe of the form in the three worlds, still remains. He knows himself to be a part of the whole.

These three processes are Death.   (17-394/5)

(3)   This entire section with which we are now engaged, called The Basic Requirements, has reference in reality to the processes of dying, to the conditions of the material world or the three worlds of incarnated service. The *restitution* of the body to the general reservoir of substance, or to service in the outer world of daily physical living, the *restoration* of the soul to its source, the soul upon its own plane or—in reverse—to full responsibility within the body, are dealt with in this first point. The *elimination* of the life principle and the consciousness aspect is dealt with in the second point, and the theme is not that of character building, as some might surmise. I touched upon character and personal qualities in my opening remarks in this section because all true understanding of the basic principles of death and life is facilitated by right action, based on right thinking, which eventuates in right character building. I seek not, however, to enlarge upon these elementary prerequisites. The processes of integration as I seek to consider them here concern the integration of the soul into the threefold body, if karma so decides, or into the kingdom of souls, if karma decrees that what we call death lies ahead of the man.   (17-391)

(4)   We shall therefore consider the three major processes to which I earlier referred; these cover three periods and lead, eventually, to other processes under the Law of Rebirth. They are:

1. *The Process of Restitution,* governing the period of withdrawal of the soul from the physical plane and from its two phenomenal aspects, the dense physical body and the etheric body. This concerns the Art of Dying.
2. *The Process of Elimination.* This governs that period of the life of the human soul after death and in the two other worlds of human evolution. It concerns the elimination of the astral-mental body by the soul, so that it is "ready to stand free in its own place."
3. *The Process of Integration,* dealing with the period wherein the liberated soul again becomes conscious of itself as the Angel of the Presence and is reabsorbed into the world of souls, thus entering into a state of reflection. Later, under the impact of the Law of Karmic Liability or Necessity, the soul again prepares itself for another descent into form.   (17-407/8)

(5)   The Law of Attraction governs the process of dying, as it governs all else in manifestation. It is the principle of coherency which, under the balanced integration of the whole body, preserves it intact, stabilises its rhythm and cyclic life processes and relates its varied parts to each other. It is the major coordinating principle within all forms, for it is the primary expression (within the soul) of the first aspect of divinity, the will aspect. This statement may surprise you, accustomed as you are to regard the Law of Attraction as an expression of the second aspect, love-wisdom. This attractive principle is found in all forms, from the tiny form of the atom to that form, the planet Earth, through which our planetary Logos expresses Himself. But if it is the principle of coherency and the cause of integration, it is also the medium through which "restitution" is brought about and by which the human soul is periodically reabsorbed into the overshadowing soul. This aspect of the Law of Attraction has, as yet, received little attention. The reason is that it concerns the highest expression of that Law, and is therefore related to the will aspect of Deity, as also the will aspect of the Monad. Only as the Shamballic force proceeds with its more direct work in the coming cycle, and men begin to discriminate (as they must and will) between self-will and the spiritual will, between determination, intention, plan, purpose, and fixed polari-

sation, will clarification come. The Law of Attraction has (as all else in manifestation) three phases or aspects, each related to the three divine aspects:

1. It relates life and form, spirit and matter—the third aspect.
2. It governs the coherent integrative process which produces forms— the second aspect.
3. It brings about the imbalance which results in the act of disintegration, thus overcoming form—as far as the human being is concerned—and brings this about in three phases to which we have given the names:
    a. *Restitution,* resulting in the dissolution of the body and the return of its elements, atoms and cells, to their originating source.
    b. *Elimination,* involving the same basic process in relation to the forces which have constituted the astral body and the mental vehicle.

   c. *Absorption,* the mode whereby the human soul is integrated into its originating source, the overshadowing, universal soul. This is an expression of the first aspect.

All these phases, rightly understood, illustrate or demonstrate the unique potency of the Law of Attraction and its relation to the Law of Synthesis, which governs the first divine aspect. Integration eventually produces synthesis. The many cyclic integrations which are carried forward in the great life cycle of an incarnating soul lead to the final synthesis of spirit and soul, which is the goal of the evolutionary process where humanity is concerned. After the third initiation, this results in the complete liberation of the man from the "pull" of substance in the three worlds and in his consequent ability to wield, with full understanding, the Law of Attraction in its various phases, as far as the creative process is involved. Other phases will then be later mastered.   (17-433/5)

(6)   The Law of Disintegration is an aspect of the Law of Death. This is the law that governs the destruction of the form in order that the indwelling life may shine forth in fullness. . . . This law breaks up the forms and the Law of Attraction draws back to primal sources the material of those forms.   (17-413)

(7)   As we well know, the blood is the life. This life activity is the factor which gathers together and holds in form all the living atoms and cells of the body. When that life thread is withdrawn by

the soul at death, the living atoms separate, the body falls apart and disintegration ensues, with the atomic lives returning to the reservoir of power, to the bosom of living matter from whence they came. (17-332)

(8) The human fear of death is primarily caused because the orientation of the kingdom of souls, the fifth kingdom in nature, has been (until relatively late in the world's cycle) towards form expression and towards the necessity of seeking experience through matter, in order eventually freely to control it. The percentage of the souls of those who are oriented away from expression in the three worlds is relatively so small, in proportion to the total number of souls demanding experience in the three worlds, that, until the cycle or era which we call the Christian, it might be stated that death reigned triumphant. Today, however, we are on the eve of seeing a complete change in this condition, owing to the fact that humanity—on a much larger scale than ever known before—is achieving a needed reorientation; the higher values and the life of the soul, as entered upon through the insistence of the mind in its higher and lower aspects, is beginning to control. This will perforce bring in a new attitude towards death; it will be regarded as a natural and desirable process, cyclically undergone. Men will eventually understand the significance of Christ's words when He said, "Render unto Caesar the things that are Caesar's and unto God the things that are God's." In the incident where those words occur He was referring to the great act of restitution which we call death. Ponder that story and see the symbolism of the soul, contained within the universal soul, as the fish within the water, and holding a coin of metal, the symbol of matter.

In one of the ancient writings the following symbolic words occur—

> *Said the Father to the son:* Go forth and take unto thyself that which is not thyself, and that which is not thine own, but which is Mine. Regard it as thine own and seek the cause of its appearance. Let it appear to be thyself. Discover thus the world of glamour, the world of deep illusion, the world of falsity. Then learn that thou hast taken that which is not the goal of soul endeavor.

> And when that moment comes in each cycle and appearance of deception and of theft, a voice

will then be heard. Obey that voice. It is the voice of that within thyself which hears My voice, a voice unheard by those who love to thieve. The order will go forth again and yet again: "Make restitution of the *stolen goods*. Learn they are not for thee." At greater intervals will come that voice again: "Make restitution of the *borrowed goods;* pay back thy debt."

And then, when all the lessons have been learnt, the voice once more will speak: "Restore with joy that which was Mine, was thine and now again is ours. Thou hast no longer need of form. Stand free."   (17-425/6)

(9)   The ideals which Christ enunciated still remain the highest yet given in the continuity of revelation, and He Himself prepared us for the emergence of those truths which will mark the time of the end and the overcoming of the last enemy, whose name is Death.   (22-243)

(10)   And *Death*—to what does this refer? Not to the death of the body or form, for that is relatively unimportant; but to the "power to relinquish," which becomes in time the characteristic of the pledged disciple. The new era is coming; the new ideals, the new civilisation, the new modes of life, of education, of religious presentation and of government are slowly precipitating and naught can stop them. They can, however, be delayed by the reactionary types of people, by the ultra-conservative and closed minds, and by those who cling with adamantine determination to their beloved theories, their dreams and their visions, their interpretations and their peculiar and oft narrow understanding of the presented ideals. *They* are the ones who can and do hold back the hour of liberation. A spiritual fluidity, a willingness to let all preconceived ideas and ideals go, as well as all beloved tendencies, cultivated habits of thought and every determined effort to make the world conform to a pattern which seems to the individual the best because, to him, the most enticing—these must all be brought under the power of death. They can be relinquished with safety and security and no fear of results, if the motive of the life is a real and lasting love of humanity. Love, true spiritual love as the soul knows it, can ever be trusted with power and opportunity and will never betray that trust. It will bring all things into line with soul vision.   (13-278/9)

(11)   Imagine the change in the human consciousness when death comes to be regarded as an act of simple and conscious relinquishing of form.   (17-427)

(12)   The art of elimination falls, therefore, into three categories:

1. As practised by those people who are purely astral in quality and constitution. These we call "kamic" people.
2. As practised by those balanced people who are integrated personalities and who are called "kama-manasic" individuals.
3. As practised by advanced people and disciples of all grades who are mainly mental in their "living focus." These are called "manasic" subjects.

The same basic rules control them all, but the emphasis differs in each case. I would have you bear in mind that where there is no physical brain and where the mind is undeveloped, the inner man finds himself practically *smothered* in an envelope of astral matter and is for a long time immersed in what we call the astral plane. The kama-manasic person has what is called the "freedom of the dual life," and finds himself possessed of a dual form which enables him to contact at will the higher levels of the astral plane and the lower levels of the mental plane. I would again remind you that there is no physical brain to register these contacts. Awareness of contact is dependent upon the innate activity of the inner man and his peculiar state of apprehension and of appreciation. The manasic person is possessed of a translucent mental vehicle with a light density which is in proportion to his freedom from desire and emotion.

These three types of people all use an eliminative process of a similar nature, but employ a different technique within the process. For the sake of clarity, it might be stated that:

1. *The kamic person* eliminates his astral body by means of attrition, and vacates it via the astral correspondence to the solar plexus centre. This attrition is brought about because all the innate desire and inherent emotion are, at this stage, related to the animal nature and the physical body — both of which are now nonexistent.
2. *The kama-manasic individual* uses two techniques. This would naturally be so because he eliminates, first of all, his astral body, and then his mental vehicle.

a. He eliminates the astral body by means of his growing desire for mental life. He withdraws gradually and steadily into the mind body, and the astral body esoterically "drops away" and finally disappears. This takes place usually unconsciously and may require quite a long time. Where, however, the man is above the average, and on the verge of becoming a manasic person, the disappearance is brought about suddenly and dynamically, and the man stands free in his mental body. This takes place consciously and rapidly.

b. He shatters the mental body by an act of the human will, and also because the soul is beginning to be slowly aware of its shadow. The inner man is therefore attracted towards the soul, though still only in a somewhat feeble manner. This process is relatively quick and is dependent upon the extent of the manasic influence.

3. *The manasic man,* focussed now in his mental body, has also two things to accomplish:

a. To dissolve and rid himself of any astral sediment which may be discolouring his translucent mental body. The so-called astral body is now practically nonexistent as a factor of expression. This he does by calling in increased light from the soul. It is soul light which, at this stage, dissolves the astral substance, just as it will be the combined light of the soul of humanity (as a whole) which will dissolve finally the astral plane—again so-called.

b. To destroy the mental body through the use of certain Words of Power. These Words are communicated to the disciple via the Ashram of his Master. They bring in soul power to a greatly enhanced extent, and produce consequently such an expansion of consciousness within the mental body that it is broken up and no longer constitutes a barrier to the inner man. He can now stand, a free son of mind, within the Ashram of his Master and "shall no more go out."   (17-487/90)

(13)   After all, death is in itself a work of restitution. It involves the work of rendering back of substance to the three worlds of substance, and doing it willingly and gladly; it involves also the restoration of the human soul to the soul from whence it emanated, and doing this in the joy of reabsorption. You must all learn to look upon death as an act of restitution . . . .   (17-389)

(14)   One of the things to remember here is that once restitu-

tion of the physical in its two aspects has taken place, the inner man is, as I have earlier said, fully conscious. The physical brain and the swirl of etheric forces (mostly somewhat disorganised in the case of the majority of men) are no longer present. These are the two factors which have led students to believe that the experiences of the man on the inner planes of the three worlds are those of a vague drifting, of a semi-conscious experience, or indicate a repetitive life, except in the case of very advanced people or disciples and initiates. But this is not the case. A man on the inner planes is not only as conscious of himself as an individual — with his own plans, life and affairs — as he was on the physical plane, but he is also conscious in the same manner of the surrounding states of consciousness. He may be glamoured by astral existence or subject to the telepathic impression of the varying thought currents emanating from the mental plane, but he is also conscious of himself and of his mind (or of the measure of manasic life developed) in a far more potent manner than when he had to work through the medium of the physical brain, when the focus of his consciousness was that of the aspirant, but anchored in the brain. His experience is far richer and fuller than he ever knew when in incarnation. If you will think this out for a little, you will realise that this necessarily would be so.   (17-494/5)

(15)   One point must be borne in mind. The words "earth to earth and dust to dust," so familiar in the burial rituals of the Occident, refer to this act of restitution and connote the return of the physical body elements to the original reservoir of matter, and of the substance of the vital form to the general etheric reservoir; the words "the spirit shall return unto God who gave it" are a distorted reference to the absorption of the soul by the universal soul. The ordinary rituals, however, fail to emphasise that it is that individualised soul, in process of reabsorption, which institutes and orders, by an act of the spiritual will, that restitution. It is forgotten in the West that this "order to restore" has been given with great frequency down the ages by every soul within a physical form; in so doing, steadily and inevitably, the first divine aspect — the Monad on its own plane — is tightening its hold upon its body of manifestation, via its reflection, the soul. Thus the will aspect comes increasingly into play until, upon the Path of Discipleship, spiritual determination is brought to its highest point of development and, upon the Path of Initiation, the will begins to function consciously. It is worth remembering, is it not, that it is in

the deliberate issuing of the command by the soul upon its own plane to its shadow in the three worlds that the soul learns to express the first and highest aspect of divinity, and this at first, and for a very long time, solely through the process of death. The difficulty at present is that relatively few people are soul-conscious, and consequently most men remain unaware of the "occult commands" of their own souls. As humanity becomes soul-conscious (and this will be one of the results of the agony of the present war), death will be seen as an "ordered" process, carried out in full consciousness and with understanding of cyclic purpose. This will naturally end the fear at present rampant, and will also arrest the tendency to suicide, evidenced increasingly in these difficult times. The sin of murder is in reality based upon the fact that it interferes with soul purpose, and not really upon the killing of a particular human physical body. That is also why war is not murder, as many well-meaning fanatics consider it; it is the destruction of forms with the beneficent intent (if one could scrutinise divine purpose) of the planetary Logos. However, it is the motives of the originators of war on the physical plane which make *them* evil. If war did not take place, the planetary life would, through what we call "acts of God," call back the souls of men on a large scale in line with His loving intention. When evil men precipitate a war, He brings good out of evil.

You can see, therefore, why the occult sciences lay the emphasis upon cyclic law, and why there is a growing interest in the Science of Cyclic Manifestation. Death appears frequently to be so purposeless; that is because the intention of the soul is not known; past development, through the process of incarnation, remains a hidden matter; ancient heredities and environments are ignored, and recognition of the voice of the soul is not yet generally developed. These are matters, however, which are on the very verge of recognition; revelation is on its way, and for that I am laying the foundation. (17-435/6)

(16) In physical death, therefore, and in the act of restitution, the withdrawing soul has to deal with the following factors:

1. The physical elemental, the integrated and coordinated life of the physical body, which is forever seeking to hold together under the attractive forces of all its component parts and their mutual interaction. This force works through a number of minor centres.

2. The etheric vehicle, which has a powerful coordinated life of its own, expressed through the seven major centres which react under astral, mental and soul impulsive energy. It works also through certain of the minor centres which are not dedicated to a response to that apsect of the man's equipment which H.P.B. states is not a principle—the dense physical mechanism.   (17-464/5)

(17)   I would, therefore, enjoin upon you the elementary fact that any healing group seeking to work along the new lines must (as a preliminary effort) seek to understand something about the factor of death to which is given the appellation of "the great restorative process" or "the great restitution." It concerns the art of wisely, correctly and with due timing, giving back the body to the source of its constituent elements and of restoring the soul to the source of its essential being. I am wording this with care because I seek to have you ponder most carefully and sanely upon the so-called enigma of death. It is an enigma to man, but not an enigma to disciples and knowers of the wisdom.   (17-390)

(18)   The theme of death, which we are now considering, must be approached by us with as much of the spirit of normalcy and of scientific investigation as we can manage. The fear complex of humanity finds its point of entrance into man's consciousness through the act of dying; failure to survive is the basic fear; and yet it is the commonest phenomenon upon the planet. Bear that in mind. The act of dying is the great universal ritual which governs our entire planetary life, but only in the human family and faintly, very faintly, in the animal kingdom is the reaction to fear found. Could you but see the etheric world as Those on the inner side of life experience and see it, you would see (going on ceaselessly and without any pause) the great planetary act of restitution. You would see a great activity proceeding within the etheric world in which the anima mundi, the animal soul and the human soul are constantly restoring the substance of all physical forms to the great reservoir of essential substance. This essential substance is as much a vital, directed unity as the world soul of which one hears so much. This interplay of the principle of death with the principle of life produces the basic activity of creation. The impulsive, directive force is the mind of God, of the planetary Logos, as He pursues His divine purposes, carrying with Him in this process all the media through which He manifests.   (17-424/5)

(19)   Through death, a great at-one-ing process is carried forward; in the "fall of a leaf" and its consequent identification with the soil on which it falls, we have a tiny illustration of this great and eternal process of at-one-ing, through becoming and dying as a result of becoming.   (17-445/6)

(20)   ... it is the destruction of the cycle of separateness as an individual upon the physical plane which we call death in the usual sense; consequently death is a process of at-one-ment.   (17-432/3)

PART XII

Death is an act of the intuition, transmitted by the soul to the personality and then acted upon in conformity to the divine will by the individual will.   *(16-599)*

PART XII

(1)   W<small>ITH THE</small> undeveloped or the average man, the soul plays a very small part in the death process, beyond the contribution of a simple soul determination to end the cycle of incarnated life, prior to another return to the physical plane. The "seeds of death" are inherent in the form nature and demonstrate as disease or as senility (using that word in its technical and not in its colloquial sense), and the soul pursues its own interests on its own plane until such time as the evolutionary process has brought about a situation wherein the integration or close relation between soul and form is so real that the soul is deeply and profoundly identified with its manifesting expression. It might be said that when this state is reached, the soul is, for the first time, truly incarnated; it is truly "descending into manifestation" and the entire soul nature is thereby involved. This is a point little emphasised or realised.

In the earlier lives of the incarnating soul and for the majority of the cycles of life experience, the soul is very slightly concerned in what is going on. The redemption of the substance of which all forms are made goes forward under natural process and the "karma of matter" is the initial governing force; this is succeeded in time by the karma generated by the fusion of soul and form, though (in the earlier stages) very little responsibility is engendered by the soul. That which occurs within the threefold soul-sheath is necessarily the result of the innate tendencies of substance itself. However, as time goes on and incarnation follows upon incarnation, the effect of the indwelling soul quality gradually evokes conscience, and—through the medium of conscience, which is the exercise of the discriminative sense, developed as the mind assumes increasing control—an awakening and finally an awakened consciousness is evoked. This demonstrates in the first instance as the sense of responsibility; it is this which gradually establishes a growing identification of the soul with its vehicle, the lower triple man. The bodies become then steadily more refined; the seeds of death and of disease are not so potent; sensitivity to inner soul realisation

93

grows until the time is reached when the initiate-disciple dies *by an act of his spiritual will or in response to group karma or to national or planetary karma.* (17-500/1)

(2) In the case of the ordinary man, where death is intended, the battle between the physical elemental and the soul is a distinctive factor; it is occultly called a "Lemurian departure"; in the case of the average citizen, where the focus of the life is in the desire nature, the conflict is between the astral elemental and the soul, and this is given the name "the death of an Atlantean"; where disciples are concerned, the conflict will be more purely mental and is oft focussed around the will-to-serve and the determination to fulfill a particular aspect of the Plan and the will-to-return in full force to the ashramic centre. Where initiates are concerned, there is no conflict, but simply a conscious and deliberate withdrawal. Curiously enough, if there appears to be a conflict, it will be between the two elemental forces then remaining in the personality: the physical elemental and the mental life. There is no astral elemental to be found in the equipment of an initiate of high standing. Desire has been completely transcended as far as the individual's own nature is involved. (17-464)

(3) There is another point upon which I wish to touch and which has relation to the eternal conflict being waged between the dualities of the dense physical body and the etheric vehicle. The physical elemental (which is the name given to the integrated life of the physical body) and the soul as it seeks to withdraw and dissolve the sumtotal of the combined energies of the etheric body, are in violent conflict and the process is often fierce and long; it is this battle which is being waged during the long or short period of coma which characterises so many death beds. Coma, esoterically speaking, is of two kinds: there is the "coma of battle" which precedes true death; there is also the "coma of restoration" which takes place when the soul has withdrawn the consciousness thread or aspect, but not the life thread, in an effort to give the physical elemental time to regain its grip upon the organism and thus to restore health. As yet, modern science does not recognise the distinction between these two aspects of coma. Later, when etheric or clairvoyant vision is more common, the quality of the coma prevailing will be known, and the elements of hope or of despair will no longer control. The friends and relations of the unconscious person will know exactly whether they are watching a great and

final withdrawal from present incarnation or simply looking on at a restorative process. In the latter case, the soul is still retaining its hold upon the physical body, via the centres, but is withstraining temporarily all energising processes. The exceptions to this withstraint are the heart centre, the spleen, and two minor centres connected with the breathing apparatus. These will remain normally energised, even if somewhat weakened in their activity; and through them control is retained. When true death is the soul's intention, then control over the spleen first of all takes place; then control over the two minor centres follows, and finally control over the heart centre supervenes and the man dies.   (17-462/3)

(4)   All these factors produce violent conflict upon the Probationary Path, which increases as the man steps upon the Path of Discipleship. The potency of the personality, dominant and being dominated, is that which induces an intense karmic activity. Events and circumstances pile fast and furiously into the experience of the disciple. His environment is of the highest quality available in the three worlds; his experience fluctuates between the extremes; he works off his karmic obligations and pays the penalty of past mistakes with great rapidity.

All this time, incarnation succeeds incarnation and the familiar process of death, intervening between cycles of experience, goes on. However, all the three deaths—physical, astral and mental—are carried out with a steadily awakening state of awareness, as the lower mind develops; the man no longer drifts—asleep and unknowing—out of the etheric, astral and mental vehicles, but each of them becomes as much an event as is physical death.

Finally the time comes when the disciple dies with deliberation and in full consciousness, and with real knowledge relinquishes his various vehicles. Steadily the soul takes control, and then the disciple brings about death through an act of the soul-will and knows exactly what he is doing.   (17-514)

(5)   In the case of highly developed human beings we often find a sense of pre-vision as to the death period; this is incident upon egoic contact and awareness of the wishes of the ego. It involves sometimes a knowledge of the very day of death, coupled to a preservation of self-determination up to the final moment of withdrawal. In the case of initiates there is much more than this. There is an intelligent understanding of the laws of abstraction and this enables the one who is making the transition to withdraw con-

sciously and in full waking awareness out of the physical body and so to function on the astral plane. This involves the preservation of continuity of consciousness so that no hiatus occurs between the sense of awareness on the physical plane and that of the after death state. The man knows himself to be as he was before, though without an apparatus whereby he can contact the physical plane. He remains aware of the states of feeling and of the thoughts of those he loves, though he cannot perceive or contact the dense physical vehicle. He can communicate with them on the astral plane or telepathically through the mind if they and he are en rapport, but communication that involves the use of the five physical senses of perception lies necessarily out of his reach. It is useful to remember, however, that astrally and mentally the interplay can be closer and more sensitive than ever before for he is freed of the handicap of the physical body. Two things, however, militate against this interplay: one is the grief and violent emotional upset of those left behind and, in the case of the average human being, the other is the man's own ignorance and bewilderment as he stands faced by what are to him new conditions, though they are really old conditions, if he could but realize it. Once men have lost the fear of death and have established an understanding of the after-death world which is not based on hallucination and hysteria or on the conclusions (oft unintelligent) of the average medium, who speaks under the control of his own thought-form (built by himself and the circle of sitters), we shall have the process of death properly controlled. The condition of those left behind will be carefully handled so that there is no loss of relationship and no false expenditure of energy.   (4-498/9)

(6)   It should be remembered that the purpose and will of the soul, the spiritual determination to be and to do, utilises the thread soul, the sutratma, the life current, as its means of expression in form. This life current differentiates into two currents or two threads when it reaches the body, and is "anchored", if I might so express it, in two locations in that body. This is symbolic of the differentiations of Atman, or Spirit, into its two reflections, soul and body. The soul, or consciousness aspect, that which makes a human being a rational, thinking entity, is "anchored" by one aspect of this thread soul to a "seat" in the brain, found in the region of the pineal gland. The other aspect of the life which animates every atom of the body and which constitutes the principle of coherence

or of integration, finds its way to the heart and is focussed or "anchored" there. From these two points, the spiritual man seeks to control the mechanism. Thus functioning on the physical plane becomes possible, and objective existence becomes a temporary mode of expression. The soul, seated in the brain, makes man an intelligent rational entity, self-conscious and self-directing; he is aware in varying degree of the world in which he lives, according to the point in evolution and the consequent development of the mechanism. That mechanism is triple in expression. There are first of all the nadis and the seven centres of force; then the nervous system in its three divisions: cerebro-spinal, sympathetic, and peripheral; and then there is the endocrine system, which might be regarded as the densest aspect or externalisation of the other two.

The soul, seated in the heart, is the life principle, the principle of self-determination, the central nucleus of positive energy by means of which all the atoms of the body are held in their right place and subordinated to the "will-to-be" of the soul. This principle of life utilises the blood stream as its mode of expression and as its controlling agency, and through the close relation of the endocrine system to the blood stream, we have the two aspects of soul activity brought together in order to make man a living, conscious, functioning entity, governed by the soul, and expressing the purpose of the soul in all the activities of daily living.

Death, therefore, is literally the withdrawal from the heart and from the head of these two streams of energy, producing consequently, complete loss of consciousness and disintegration of the body. Death differs from sleep in that *both* streams of energy are withdrawn. In sleep only the thread of energy, which is anchored in the brain is withdrawn, and when this happens the man becomes unconscious. By this we mean that his consciousness or sense of awareness is focussed elsewhere. His attention is no longer directed towards things tangible and physical but is turned upon another world of being and becomes centred in another apparatus or mechanism. In death, both the threads are withdrawn or unified in the life thread. Vitality ceases to penetrate through the medium of the blood stream and the heart fails to function just as the brain fails to record, and thus silence settles down. The house is empty. Activity ceases except that amazing and immediate activity which is the prerogative of matter itself and which expresses itself in the process of decomposition.   (4-495/7)

(7)   When the disciple or the initiate is identifying himself with the soul, and when the antahkarana is built by means of the life principle, then the disciple passes out of the control of this universal, natural law and uses or discards the body at will—at the demand of the spiritual will or through recognition of the necessities of the Hierarchy or the purposes of Shamballa.   (17-501)

(8)   In the matter of death, this freewill has, in the last analysis, a definite relation to the soul; the will of the soul is either consciously or unconsciously followed, where the decision of death is concerned, and this idea carries with it many implications which students would do well to ponder.   (17-248)

(9)   . . . suffice it to say that the three major diseases of humanity to which reference has been made take their toll of disciples, particularly in bringing about the liberation of the soul from its vehicle. They are, however—little as it may appear—controlled in these cases from soul levels, and the departure is planned to take place as a result of soul decision, and not as a result of the efficiency of the disease.   (17-121)

(10)   The processes of abstraction are (as you may thus see) connected with the life aspect, are set in motion by an act of the spiritual will, and constitute the "resurrection principle which lies hidden in the work of the Destroyer," as an old esoteric saying expresses it. The lowest manifestation of this principle is to be seen in the process of what we call Death—which is in reality a means of abstracting the life principle, informed by consciousness, from the form or the bodies in the three worlds.

          Thus, the great synthesis emerges, and destruction, death, and dissolution are in reality naught but life processes. Abstraction is indicative of process, progress and development.   (18-163)

(11)   Two major thoughts will serve to clarify the issue of death with which we are now concerned: First, the great dualism ever present in manifestation. Each of the dualities has its own expression, is governed by its own laws, and seeks its own objectives. But—in time and space—they merge their interests for the benefit of both, and together produce the appearance of a unity. Spirit-matter, life-appearance, energy-force—each have their own emanating aspect; they each have a relation to each other; each have a mutual temporary objective, and thus in unison produce the eternal flux, the cyclic ebb and flow of life in manifestation. In this

process of relationship between Father-Spirit and Mother-Matter the son comes into being, and during the child stage carries on his life processes within the aura of the mother, identified with her yet forever seeking to escape from her domination. As maturity is reached, the problem intensifies, and the "pull" of the Father begins slowly to offset the possessive attitude of the mother, until finally the hold of matter, or of the mother, over her son (the soul) is finally broken. The son, the Christ-child, released from the guardianship and clinging hands of the mother, comes to know the Father. I am talking to you in symbols.

Second: All the processes of incarnation, of life in form and of restitution (by the activity of the principle of death), of matter to matter, and soul to soul, are carried forward under the great universal Law of Attraction. Can you picture the time when the process of death, clearly recognised and welcomed by the man, could be described by him in the simple phrase, "The time has come when my soul's attractive force requires that I relinquish and restore my body to the place from whence it came"? Imagine the change in the human consciousness when death comes to be regarded as an act of simple and conscious relinquishing of form, temporarily taken for two specific objectives:

a. To gain control in the·three worlds.
b. To give opportunity to the substance of the forms thus "stolen or borrowed or rightly appropriated," according to the stage of evolution, to reach a higher point of perfection through the impact upon it of life, via the soul.

These are significant thoughts. They have been expressed before, but have been discarded as symbolic, as comforting or as wishful thinking. I present them to you as factual in nature, as unavoidable in practice, and as familiar a technique and process as those activities, (rhythmic and cyclic in nature) which govern the average man's life—rising and retiring, eating and drinking, and all the periodic affairs which he is accustomed to pursue.   (17-426/8)

(12)   It is important to note that it is under the basic and fundamental Law of Attraction that the Art of Dying is carried forward, and that it is the love aspect, the second aspect of divinity, which does the attracting. I exclude cases of sudden death. There the activity is the result of the destroyer, or the first divine aspect. There the condition is different; individual karmic necessity may not be involved at all, and reasons of group conditioning and of

great obscurity may lie behind such a happening. So obscure is the subject at this time that I shall not attempt to elucidate. You do not know enough about the Law of Karma, about karmic group involvement, or about relationships and obligations established in past lives. When I say, for instance, that on occasion the "soul may leave the door of protection open so that the forces of death itself may enter anew, having no focal point behind the door" in order "more rapidly to obliterate past penalties due," you can see how obscure this whole matter can be.

In all that I am here writing, I am dealing simply with normal death processes—death which comes as the result of disease, old age, or the imposed will of the soul which has completed a designed cycle of experience and is using normal channels to attain projected ends. Death in these cases is *normal,* and this humanity needs to grasp with greater patience, understanding and hope.

Under the Law of Attraction, the soul, at the close of a life cycle, and with full intention, exerts its attractive power in such a manner that it offsets the attractive power inherent in matter itself. This a clear definition of the basic cause of death. Where no soul contact has been consciously established, as in the case of the majority of people at this time, death comes as an unexpected or sadly anticipated event. Yet—*it is a true soul activity.* This is the first great spiritual concept to be proclaimed as the fear of death is combatted. Death is carried forward under this Law of Attraction, and consists in the steady and scientific abstraction of the vital body out of the dense physical body, leading eventually to an elimination of all soul contact in the three worlds.   (17-471/2)

(13)   The Law of Attraction breaks up the forms and draws back to primal sources the material of those forms, prior to rebuilding them anew. On the path of evolution the effects of this law are well-known, not only in the destruction of discarded vehicles, but in the breaking up of the forms in which great ideals are embodied. . . . All eventually break under the working of this law.

Its workings are more apparent to the average human mind in its manifestations at this time on the physical plane. We can trace the connection between the atmic (spiritual) and the physical plane—demonstrating on the lower plane as the Law of Sacrifice and Death—but its effect can be seen on all five planes as well. It is the law which destroys the final sheath that separates the perfected soul.   (17-415)

(14)   Life is approached from the angle of the Observer, and not from that of a participator in actual experiment and experience in the three worlds (physical—emotional—mental) . . . if they are initiated disciples they are increasingly unaware of the activities and reactions of their personalities, because certain aspects of the lower nature are now so controlled and purified that they have dropped below the threshold of consciousness and have entered the world of instinct; therefore, there is no more awareness of them than a man asleep is conscious of the rhythmic functioning of his sleeping physical vehicle. This is a deep and largely unrealized truth. It is related to the entire process of death, and might be regarded as one of the definitions of death; it holds the clue to the mysterious words "the reservoir of life." Death is in reality un-consciousness of that which may be functioning in some form or another, but in a form of which the spiritual entity is totally unaware. The reservoir of life is the place of death, and this is the first lesson the disciple learns . . . .   (17-445)

(15)   This—as far as you can at this time grasp—concerns primarily the creative will as it:

1. Initiates manifestation, and conditions that which is created.
2. Brings about eventual fulfillment.
3. Overcomes death or differentiation.

All initiates must and eventually do express dynamic, creative will, a focussed purpose which expresses only the will-to-good and also that sustained effort which brings fulfillment. I would remind you here that *sustained effort is the seed of synthesis, the cause of achievement and that which finally overcomes death.* Death is re-ally deterioration in time and space and is due to the tendency of matter-spirit to isolate itself, whilst in manifestation (from the standpoint of consciousness). This sustained effort of the Logos is what keeps all forms in manifestation and preserves even the life aspect as the integrating factor in form building and—which is equally an act of the sustaining will—can abstract or with-draw the life consciousness intact at the close of a cycle of mani-festation.   (16-614/5)

(16)   You will by now have realised that we have discussed the fact of death as it has affected the physical body (a most familiar happening) and also the astral or mental sheaths—those aggregations of conditioned energy with which we are not so objec-tively familiar but which even psychology admits exist and which

we believe must disintegrate or disappear with the death of the physical body. Has it, however, occurred to you that the major aspect of death with which a human being is ultimately concerned is the death of the personality? I am not here speaking in abstract terms, as do all esotericists when they work at the negation of quality or of the qualities which characterise the personal self. They speak of "killing out" this or that quality, of completely suppressing the "lower self," and similar phrases. Here I am speaking of the literal destruction, dissolution, dissipation or final dispersal of that beloved and well-known personal self.

It must be borne in mind that the life of a personality falls into the following stages:

1. Its slow and gradual construction over a long period of time. For many cycles of incarnations, a man is not a personality. He is just a member of the mass.
2. The conscious identification of the soul with the personality during this stage is practically nonexistent. The aspect of the soul which is concealed within the sheaths is for a long, long period dominated by the life of those sheaths, only making its presence felt through what is called "the voice of conscience." However, as time goes on, the active intelligent life of the person is gradually enhanced and coordinated by the energy which streams from the knowledge petals of the egoic lotus, or from the intelligent perceptive nature of the soul on its own plane. This produces eventually the integration of the three lower sheaths into one functioning whole. The man is then a personality.
3. The personality life of the now coordinated individual persists for a large number of lives, and also falls into three phases:
   a. The phase of a dominant aggressive personality life, basically conditioned by its ray type, selfish in nature and very individualistic.
   b. A transitional phase wherein a conflict rages between personality and soul. The soul begins to seek liberation from form life and yet—in the last analysis—the personality is dependent upon the life principle, conferred by the soul. Wording it otherwise, the conflict between the soul ray and the personality ray starts and the war is on between two focussed aspects of energy. This conflict terminates at the third initiation.

c. The control by the soul is the final phase, leading to the death and destruction of the personality. This death begins when the personality, the Dweller on the Threshold, stands before the Angel of the Presence. The light of the solar Angel then obliterates the light of matter.   (17-505/7)

(17)   *The Elimination of the Personality Thoughtform*

In dealing with this subject (and it can only be done very briefly) two things must be borne in mind:

1. That we are considering solely an idea in the mind of the soul and dealing with the basic fact of the illusion which has controlled the entire cycle of incarnation and so held the soul a prisoner to form. To the soul, the personality connotes two things:
    a. The soul's capacity for identification with form; this is first of all realized by the soul when the personality is beginning to react to a measure of real integration.
    b. An opportunity for initiation.
2. That the elimination of the thoughtform of the personality, which is consummated at the third initiation, is a great initiation for the soul on its own plane. For this reason, the third initiation is regarded as the first major initiation, since the two previous initiations have very little effect upon the soul and only affect the incarnated soul, the "fragment" of the whole.

These are facts which are little realized and seldom emphasized in any of the literature hitherto published. The emphasis up till now has been upon the initiations as they affect the disciple in the three worlds. But I am specifically dealing with the initiations as they affect or do not affect the soul, overshadowing its reflection, the personality, in the three worlds. What I have said, therefore, will have little meaning for the average reader.

From the angle of the personal self, regarding itself as the Dweller on the Threshold, the attitude or state of mind has been inadequately portrayed as one of complete obliteration in the light of the soul; the glory of the Presence, transmuted by the Angel, is such that the personality completely disappears, with its demands and its aspirations. Naught is left but the shell, the sheath, and the instrument through which the solar light can pour for the helping of humanity. This is true to a certain degree, but is only—in the last analysis—man's attempt to put into words the transmuting and the transfiguring effect of the third initiation, which cannot be done.

Infinitely more difficult is the attempt I am here making to depict the attitude and the reactions of the soul, the one self, the Master in the heart, as it recognises the stupendous fact of its own essential liberation and realises, once and for all, that it is now incapable of responding in any way to the lower vibrations of the three worlds, as transmitted to the soul by its instrument of contact, the personality form. That form is now incapable of such transmission.

The second reaction of the soul, once this realisation has been focussed and admitted, is that—having achieved freedom—that freedom now conveys its own demands:

1. For a life of service in the three worlds, so familiar and now so completely transcended.
2. An overshadowing sense of outgoing love towards those who are, as yet, seeking liberation.
3. A recognition of the essential triangle which has now become the centre of the conceptual life of the soul:

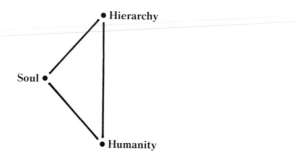

The soul now vibrates between the two points or pairs of opposites and acts as an invocative and evocative centre.

None of the above realizations may be registered in the brain consciousness or in the mind of the illumined personality. Theoretically, some dim vision of the inherent possibilities may be sensed, but the consciousness is no longer that of the serving disciple in the three worlds, using mind, emotions and physical body to carry out behest and hierarchical intent, as far as may be. That has disappeared with the death of the personality consciousness. The consciousness is now that of the soul itself, aware of no separation, instinctively active, spiritually obsessed by the plans of the Kingdom of God, and completely free from the lure or the faintest control of matter-form; the soul is, however, still responsive to and immersed in substance-energy, and its higher correspondence is still functioning on the levels of the cosmic physical plane—the buddhic, atmic, monadic and logoic planes.

What then must take place if the life of the soul is to be full and complete and so thoroughly inclusive that the three worlds form part of its area of awareness and its field of service? The only way in which I can make clear to you what the soul must do after the third initiation is to sum it up in two ways:

First: The soul now becomes a conscious creator because the third aspect—developed and mastered through experience in the three worlds during the long cycle of incarnations—has reached a point of perfected activity. Putting it technically: the energy of the knowledge petals and the energy of the love petals are now so actively fused and blended that two of the inner petals, surrounding the jewel in the lotus, are no longer acting as veils to that jewel. I am here speaking symbolically. Because of this happening, the death or the elimination of the personality is the first activity in the drama of conscious creation, and the first form created by the soul is a substitute for the personality. Thus an instrument for service in the three worlds is created. This time, however, it is an instrument with no life, no desire, no ambition and no power of thought of its own. It is only a sheath of substance, animated by soul life but—at the same time—responsive to and suited to the period, race and the environing conditions wherein the creating soul chooses to work. Think this statement out and emphasize the words "suited to."

Second: The soul then prepares itself for the coming fourth initiation. This is basically a monadic experience and results—as you know—in the disappearance or destruction of the soul vehicle or causal body, and the establishment, therefore, of a direct relation between the monad on its own plane and the newly created personality, via the antahkarana.

These two points are given to you for the first time in the sequential giving out of the occult teaching; hints have, however, prepared the way for these two facts. Information has also been given anent the mayavirupa through which the Master works and contacts the three worlds and which He deliberately creates in order to serve His purposes and plans. It is a definite substitute for the personality and can only be created when the old personality (built and developed during the cycle of incarnation) has been eliminated. I prefer the word "eliminated" to the word "destroyed." The *structure*—at the time of elimination—persists, but its separative life has gone.

If you will think clearly about this statement, you will see that a very complete integration is now possible. The personality life has been absorbed; the personality form is still felt, but it persists without any real life of its own; this means that it can now be the recipient of energies and forces, needed by the working initiate or Master in order to carry on the work of salvaging humanity. Students would find it of value to study the three "appearances of the Christ" as recorded in the Gospel story:

1. His transfigured appearance upon the Mount of Transfiguration. That episode depicts symbolically the radiant soul, and also the three vacated bodies of the personality, and hints also at a future building of a vehicle of manifestation. St. Peter says, "Lord, let us here build three huts" or tabernacles.
2. His appearance as truth itself (silent yet present) before the bar or judgment seat of Pilate—repudiated by the world of men but recognized by the Hierarchy.
3. His radiant appearances after the resurrection initiation:
    a. To the woman at the sepulchre—symbolizing His contact with Humanity.
    b. To the two disciples on the way to Emmaus—symbolizing His contact with Hierarchy.
    c. To the twelve disciples in the upper chamber—symbolizing His contact with the Council Chamber of the Lord of the World at Shamballa.

You can thus see the factual nature of the results to which I earlier referred in this instruction. The disciple who has eliminated (in the technical sense as well as in the mystical sense) the hold of the personality has now the "freedom of the Ashram," as it is called; he can move at will among his fellow disciples and initiates. There will be nothing in his vibratory life or his quality which can disturb the rhythm of the Ashram; there will be nothing to call forth the "calming intervention" of the Master, as is frequently the case during the earlier stages of discipleship; nothing can now interfere with those higher contacts and spheres of influence which have hitherto been sealed to the disciple because of the intrusion of his own personality.   (17-515/20)

(18)   You can see, therefore, why it is that those who have succeded in building the antahkarana, the rainbow bridge between the Monad and the personality, have established a contact (non-existent in the average man) between the Monad, the Source of Life, and the personality—the expression of that Life in objectivity. The Monad then, and not the soul, controls the cycles of outward expression, and the initiate then dies at will and according to plan or the necessities of the work. This, of course, refers only to initiates of high degree.   (17-642)

PART XIII

And then a Word sounds forth. The descended, radiating point of light ascends, responsive to the dimly heard recalling note, attracted to its emanating source. This man calls death and this the soul calls life. *(17-469)*

PART XIII

(1) $\quad$ I WISH you could get a picture (symbolically considered) of a man who is in full incarnation and rooted in his phase of experience, and of a man who is withdrawing from that experience. It connotes a repetition on a tiny scale of the great planetary processes of involution and evolution; it concerns those activities which produce a focussing or a polarisation in one of two directions; it resembles what might be regarded as a process of pouring in life and light into a vessel upon the physical plane, or an intensification of the radiation of that life and light of so potent a nature that under the evocative power of the soul they are both withdrawn and gathered up into the centre of life and light from whence they originally came. I have here given you (could you but recognise it) a definition of initiation, but one of a somewhat unusual phrasing. Perhaps some lines from the *Manual of Death* which is to be found in the hierarchical archives would prove explanatory to you, and might aid you in gaining a new perspective upon death. This manual has in it what are called the "Formulas preceding Pralaya". These deal with all the death or abstraction processes, covering the death of all forms, whether it be the death of an ant, a man or a planet. The formulas concern only the two aspects of life and light—the first conditioned by Sound and the second by the Word. The writing which I have in mind concerns the light, and the Word which abstracts it from the form or focusses it within the form.

> "Bear in mind, O Chela, that within the known spheres naught is but light responsive to the WORD. Know that that light descends and concentrates itself; know that from its point of chosen focus, it lightens its own sphere; know too that light ascends and leaves in darkness that which it—in time and space—illumined. This descending and ascension men call life, existence and decease; this We Who tread the Lighted Way call death, experience and life.
>
> Light which descends anchors itself upon the plane of temporary appearance. Seven threads it

outward puts, and seven rays of light pulsate along
these threads. Twenty-one lesser threads are radi-
ated thence, causing the forty-nine fires to glow and
burn. Upon the plane of manifested life, the word
goes forth: Behold! A man is born.

As life proceeds, the quality of light appears;
dim and murky it may be, or radiant, bright and
shining. Thus do the points of light within the Flame
pass and repass; they come and go. This men call
life; they call it true existence. They thus delude
themselves yet serve the purpose of their souls and
fit into the greater Plan.

And then a Word sounds forth. The descended,
radiating point of light ascends, responsive to the
dimly heard recalling note, attracted to its emanating source. This man calls death and this the soul
calls life.

The Word retains the light in life; the Word
abstracts the light, and only *That* is left which is the
Word itself. That Word is Light. That Light is Life,
and Life is God."

The manifestation of the etheric body in time and space has in it
what has been esoterically called "two moments of brilliance."
These are, first, the moment prior to physical incarnation, when
the descending light (carrying life) is focussed in all its intensity
around the physical body and sets up a rapport with the innate
light of matter itself, to be found in every atom of substance. This
focussing light will be found to concentrate itself in seven areas of
its ring-pass-not, thus creating seven major centres which will
control its expression and its existence upon the outer plane, esoterically speaking. This is a moment of great radiance; it is almost
as if a point of pulsating light burst into flame, and as if within that
flame seven points of intensified light took shape. This is a high
point in the experience of taking incarnation, and precedes physical birth by a very short period of time. It is that which brings on
the birth hour. The next phase of the process, as seen by the
clairvoyant, is the stage of interpenetration, during which "the
seven become the twenty-one and then the many"; the light substance, the energy aspect of the soul, begins to permeate the physical body, and the creative work of the etheric or vital body is
completed. The first recognition of this upon the physical plane is

the "sound" uttered by the newborn infant. It climaxes the process. The act of creation by the soul is now complete; a new light shines forth in a dark place.

The second moment of brilliance comes in reverse of this process and heralds the period of restitution and the final abstraction of its own intrinsic energy by the soul. The prison house of the flesh is dissolved by the withdrawing of the light and life. The forty-nine fires within the physical organism die down; their heat and light are absorbed into the twenty-one minor points of light; these, in their turn, are absorbed by the major seven centres of energy. Then the "Word of Return" is uttered, and the consciousness aspect, the quality nature, the light and energy of the incarnating man, are withdrawn into the etheric body. The life principle withdraws, likewise, from the heart. There follows a brilliant flaring-up of pure electric light, and the "body of light" finally breaks all contact with the dense physical vehicle, focusses for a short period in the vital body, and then disappears. The act of restitution is accomplished. This entire process of the focussing of the spiritual elements in the etheric body, with the subsequent abstraction and consequent dissipation of the etheric body, would be greatly hastened by the substitution of cremation for burial.   (17-467/70)

(2)   It has been asked: What is the Tibetan's attitude towards cremation, and under what conditions should cremation be followed? It is a fortunate and happy thing that cremation is becoming increasingly the rule. Before so very long, burial in the ground will be against the law and cremation will be enforced, and this as a health and sanitation measure. Those unhealthy, psychic spots, called cemeteries, will eventually disappear, just as ancestor worship is passing out, both in the Orient—with its ancestor cults—and the Occident with its equally foolish cult of hereditary position.

By the use of fire, all forms are dissolved; the quicker the human physical vehicle is destroyed, the quicker is its hold upon the withdrawing soul broken. A great deal of nonsense has been told in current theosophical literature about the time equation in relation to the sequential destruction of the subtle bodies. It should be stated, however, that the moment that *true* death is scientifically established (by the orthodox doctor in charge of the case), and it has been ascertained that no spark of life remains in the physical body, cremation is then possible. This complete or true death eventuates when the thread of consciousness and the thread of life are completely withdrawn from the head and the heart. At the same time, reverence and an unhurried attitude have their rightful place in the process. The family of the dead person need a few hours in which to adjust themselves to the fact of the imminent disappearance of the outer and usually loved form; due care must also be given to the formalities required by the state or the municipality. This time element has reference mainly to those who are left behind, to the living and not to the dead. The claim that the etheric body must not be rushed into the cremating flames, and the belief that it must be left to drift around for a stated period of several days, have also no true basis at all. There is no etheric need for delay. When the inner man withdraws from his physical vehicle he withdraws simultaneously from the etheric body. It is true that the etheric body is apt to linger for a long time on the "field of emanation" when the physical body is interred, and it will frequently persist until complete disintegration of the dense body has taken place. The process of mummifying, as practised in Egypt, and of embalming, as practised in the West, have been responsible for the perpetuation of the etheric body, sometimes for centuries. This is particularly the case when the mummy or embalmed person was of an evil character during life; the hovering etheric body is then often "possessed" by an evil entity or evil force. This is the cause of the attacks and the disasters which often dog the steps of those who discover ancient tombs and their inhabitants, ancient mummies, and bring them and their possessions to light. Where cremation is the rule, there is not only the immediate destruction of the physical body and its restitution to the fount of substance, but the vital body is also promptly dissolved and its forces swept away by the current of flame into the reservoir of vital energies. Of that reservoir it has ever been an inherent part, either in form or in a formless condition. After death and cremation these forces still exist but are absorbed into the *analogous* whole. Ponder on this statement, for it will give you the clue to the creative work of the human spirit. If delay is necessary from family feeling or municipal requirements, cremation should follow death within thirty-six hours; where no reason for delay exists, cremation can be rightly permitted in twelve hours. It is wise, however, to wait twelve hours in order to ensure *true* death. (17-483/5)

(3)   Occultly speaking, cremation is needed for two main reasons. It hastens the release of the subtle vehicles (still en-

shrouding the soul) from the etheric body, thus bringing about the release in a few hours instead of a few days; it also is a much needed means for bringing about the purification of the astral plane and for arresting the "downward moving" tendency of desire which so greatly handicaps the incarnating soul. It can find no point of focus, because essentially fire repels the form-making aspect of desire and is a major expression of divinity with which the astral plane has no true relation, being created entirely by the human soul and not the divine soul. "Our God is a consuming fire" is the statement in the Bible which refers to the first divine aspect, the aspect of the destroyer, releasing the life. "God is love" connotes the second aspect and portrays God as incarnated existence. "God is a jealous God" is an expression indicating God as form, circumscribed and limited, self-centered and not outgoing. The destroying Sound; the attracting Word; the individualised Speech!

At the time of death, speech fades out as the Word sounds forth and restitution is enforced; later, the Word is no longer heard as the Sound obliterates or absorbs it, and there is then complete elimination of all that interferes with Sound. Silence then supervenes and the Sound itself is no longer heard; complete peace follows the act of final integration. Here, in esoteric phraseology, the entire process of death is described.   (17-470/1)

(4)   It would perhaps be wise if we took this tenth Law somewhat in detail, where possible, so as to arrive at the synthesis which it is intended to convey: we will thus gain some realisation that death itself is a part of the creative process of synthesising. It is essential that new ideas and a new approach to the entire problem of dying are inaugurated.

> *Hearken, O Disciple, to the call which comes from the Son to the Mother, and then obey.*

Even whilst we realise from the context that this refers to the discarding of the physical body, it is useful to remember that this form of wording can signify much more than that. It can be interpreted to mean the entire relation of soul and personality, and to involve the prompt obedience of the Mother (the personality) to the Son (the soul). Without his prompt obedience, involving as it does the recognition of the informing Voice, the personality will remain deaf to the call of the soul to relinquish the body. No habitual response has been developed. I would ask you to ponder on the implications.

I am, I know, recapitulating when I point out that the Mother aspect is the material aspect and the soul—on its own plane—is the Son. This injunction, therefore, concerns the relation of matter and soul, and thus lays the foundation for all the relationships which the disciple has to learn to recognize. Obedience is not here enforced; it is contingent upon hearing; then obedience follows as the next development. This is an easier process, little as you may think it. This distinction, relative to the process of obedience, is interesting because the process of *learning by hearing* is always slow and is one of the qualities or aspects of the stage of orientation. *Learning by sight* is definitely connected with the Path of Discipleship, and any who wish to become wise and true workers must learn to distinguish between the hearers and those who see. A realisation of the difference would lead to basic changes in technique. In the one case, you are working with those who are definitely under the influence and control of the Mother, and who need to be trained to see. In the other, you are dealing with those who have heard and who are developing the spiritual correspondence of sight. They are therefore susceptible to the vision.

> *The Word goes forth that form has served its purpose.*

This word, or this "spiritual proclamation" of the soul, may have a twofold purpose: it may produce death, or it may simply result in a withdrawal of the soul from its instrument, the threefold personality. This might consequently result in leaving the form uninformed and without any dweller in the body. When this happens the personality (and by this I mean the physical, astral and mental man) will continue to function. If it is of a high grade quality, very few people will realise that the soul is absent. This frequently happens in old age or serious illness, and it may persist for years. It sometimes happens where infants are concerned, and you then have either death or imbecility, as there has been no time to train the lower personality vehicles. A little thinking along the lines of this "forthgoing Word" will throw much light on circumstances which are regarded as baffling, and on states of consciousness which have hitherto constituted almost insoluable problems.

> *The principle of mind then organises itself and then repeats the Word. The waiting form responds and drops away.*

In the aspect of death here dealt with it is the mind which acts as the agent of authority, transmitting to the brain (where the thread of consciousness is located) the instruction to vacate. This is then passed on by the man in the body to the heart (where the life thread is anchored), and then—as you well know—the process of withdrawal begins. What transpires in those timeless moments prior to death no one as yet knows, for no one has returned to tell us. If they had done so, the question is: Would they have been believed? The probability is that they would not.

The first paragraph of this Law X deals with the passing out from the body (meaning the form aspect of the threefold lower man) of the average intelligent aspirant, looking at this law from one of its lowest correspondences; however, under the same Law of Correspondences, the death of all men, from the lowest type of man up to and inclusive of the aspirant, is basically distinguished by the same identical process; the difference exists in the degree of consciousness evidenced—consciousness of process and intention. The result is the same in all cases:

The soul stands free.

This moment of true freedom can be brief and fleeting as in the case of the undeveloped man, or it can be of long duration, according to the usefulness of the aspirant upon the inner planes; with this I have earlier dealt and have no need to repeat myself here. Progressively, as the urges and influences of the three lower levels of consciousness weaken their hold, the period of dissociation becomes longer and longer, and is characterised by a developing clarity of thought and by a recognition of essential being, and this in progressive stages. This clarity and progress may not be brought through into full realisation or expression when rebirth again takes place, for the limitations imposed by the dense physical body are excessive; nevertheless, each life sees a steady growth in sensitivity, and also the storing-up of esoteric information, using the word "esoteric" to signify all that does not concern normal form life or the average consciousness of man in the three worlds.   (17-680/3)

(5)   What is the result of this withdrawal, or rather what causes that something which we call death or pralaya? As we are strictly pursuing the text-book style in this treatise, we will continue our methods of tabulation. The withdrawal of the etheric double of a man, a planet, and a system is brought about by the following causes:

a. The cessation of desire. This should be the result of all evolutionary process. *True* death, under the law, is brought about by the attainment of the objective, and hence by the cessation of aspiration. This, as the perfected cycle draws to its close, will be true of the individual human being, of the Heavenly Man, and of the Logos Himself.

b. By the slowing down and gradual cessation of the cyclic rhythm, *the adequate vibration is achieved,* and the work accomplished. When the vibration or note is perfectly felt or sounded it causes (at the point of synthesis with other vibrations) the utter shattering of the forms.

Motion is characterised, as we know, by three qualities:
1. Inertia,
2. Mobility,
3. Rhythm.

These three are experienced in just the above sequence and presuppose a period of slow activity, succeeded by one of extreme movement. This middle period produces incidentally (as the true note and rate is sought) cycles of chaos, of experiment, of experience and of comprehension. Following on these two degrees of motion (which are characteristic of the atom, Man, of the Heavenly Man or group, and of the Logos or the Totality) comes a period of rhythm and of stabilisation wherein the point of balance is achieved. By the force of balancing the pairs of opposites, and thus producing equilibrium, pralaya is the inevitable sequence.

c. By the severing of the physical from the subtler body on the inner planes, through the shattering of the web. This has a threefold effect:

First. The life that had animated the physical form (both dense and etheric) and which had its starting point in the permanent atom and from thence "prevaded the moving and the unmoving" (in God, the Heavenly Man, and the human being, as well as in the atom of matter) is withdrawn entirely within the atom upon the plane of abstraction. This "plane of abstraction" is a different one for the entities involved:

a. For the physical permanent atom, it is the atomic level.
b. For man, it is the causal vehicle.
c. For the Heavenly Man, it is the second plane of monadic life, His habitat.
d. For the Logos, it is the plane of Adi.

All these mark the points for the disappearance of the unit into pralaya. We need here to remember that it is always pralaya when viewed from *below*. From the higher vision, that sees the subtler continuously overshadowing the dense when not in objective manifestation, pralaya is simply subjectivity, and is not that "which is not," but simply that which is esoteric.

Second. The etheric double of a man, a planetary Logos, and a solar Logos, being shattered, becomes nonpolarised as regards its indweller, and permits therefore of escape. It is (to word it otherwise) no longer a source of attraction, nor a focal magnetic point. It becomes non-magnetic, and the great Law of Attraction ceases to control it; hence disintegration is the ensuing condition of the form. The Ego ceases to be attracted by its form on the physical plane, and, proceeding to inbreathe, withdraws its life from out of the sheath. The cycle draws to a close, the experiment has been made, the objective (a relative one from life to life and from incarnation to incarnation) has been achieved, and there remains nothing more to desire; the Ego, or the thinking entity, loses interest therefore in the form, and turns his attention inward. His polarisation changes, and the physical is eventually dropped.

The planetary Logos likewise in His greater cycle (the synthesis or the aggregate of the tiny cycles of the cells of His body) pursues the same course; He ceases to be attracted downward or outward, and turns His gaze within; He gathers inward the aggregate of the smaller lives within His body, the planet, and severs connection. Outer attraction ceases and all gravitates towards the centre instead of scattering to the periphery of His body.

In the system, the same process is followed by the solar Logos; from His high place of abstraction, He ceases to be attracted by His body of manifestation. He withdraws His interest and the two pairs of opposites, the spirit and the matter of the vehicle, dissociate. With this dissociation the solar system, that "Son of Necessity," or of desire, ceases to be, and passes out of objective existence.

Third. This leads finally, to the scattering of the atoms of the etheric body into their primordial condition. The subjective life, the synthesis of will and love taking active form, is withdrawn. The partnership is dissolved. The form then breaks up; the magnetism that has held it in coherent shape is no longer present, and dissipation is complete. Matter persists, but the *form* no longer persists.

The work of the second Logos ends, and the divine incarnation of the Son is concluded. But the faculty or inherent quality of matter also persists, and at the end of each period of manifestation, matter (though distributed again into its primal form) is active intelligent matter plus the gain of objectivity, and the increased radiatory and latent activity which it has gained through experience. Let us illustrate: The matter of the solar system, when undifferentiated, was active intelligent matter, and that is all that can be predicated of it. This active intelligent matter was matter qualified by an earlier experience, and coloured by an earlier incarnation. *Now* this matter is *in form,* the solar system is not in pralaya but in objectivity,—this objectivity having in view the addition of another quality to the logoic content, that of love and wisdom. Therefore at the next solar pralaya, at the close of the one hundred years of Brahma, the matter of the solar system will be coloured by active intelligence, and by active love. This means literally that the aggregate of solar atomic matter will eventually vibrate to another key than it did at the first dawn of manifestation.

We can work this out in connection with the planetary Logos and the human unit, for the analogy holds good. We have a correspondence on a tiny scale in the fact that each human life period sees a man taking a more evolved physical body of a greater responsiveness, tuned to a higher key, of more adequate refinement, and vibrating to a different measure. In these three thoughts lies much information, if they are carefully studied and logically extended.

d. By the transmutation of the violet into the blue. This we cannot enlarge on. We simply make the statement, and leave its working out to those students whose karma permits and whose intuition suffices.

e. By the withdrawal of the life, the form should gradually dissipate. The reflex action here is interesting to note, for the greater Builders and Devas who are the active agents during manifestation, and who hold the form in coherent shape, transmuting, applying and circulating the pranic emanations, likewise lose their attraction to the matter of the form, and turn their attention elsewhere. On the path of out-breathing (whether human, planetary or logoic) these building devas (on the same Ray as the unit desiring manifestation, or on a complementary Ray) are attracted by his will and desire, and perform their office of construction. On the path of inbreathing (whether human, planetary or logoic) they are no longer attracted, and the form begins to dissipate. They withdraw their interest and the forces (likewise entities) who are the agents of destruction, carry on their necessary work of breaking up the form; they scatter it—as it is occultly expressed—to "The four winds of Heaven," or to the regions of the four breaths,—a fourfold separation and distribution. A hint is here given for careful consideration.

Though no pictures have been drawn of death bed scenes nor of the dramatic escape of the palpitating etheric body from the centre in the head, as might have been anticipated, yet some of the rules and purposes governing this withdrawal have been mentioned. We have seen how the aim of each life (whether human, planetary or solar) should be the effecting and the carrying out of a definite purpose. This purpose is the development of a more adequate form for the use of the spirit; and when this purpose is achieved then the Indweller turns his attention away, and the form disintegrates, having served his need. This is not always the case in every human life nor even in each planetary cycle. The mystery of the moon is the mystery of failure. This leads, when comprehended, to a life of dignity and offers an aim worthy of our best endeavour. When this angle of truth is universally recognised, as it will be when the intelligence of the race suffices, then evolution will proceed with certainty, and the failures be less numerous.   (3-129/33)

(6)   To turn now to another aspect of our theme. There are, speaking in the larger sense, three major death episodes.

There is, first of all, the constant recurrence of the fact of physical death. This is familiar to all of us through its extreme frequency, could we but realise it. This recognition would rapidly eliminate the present fear of death. There is then the "second death" spoken of in the Bible, which is in this present planetary cycle associated with the death of all astral control over the human being. In the larger sense, this second death is consummated at the fourth initiation, when even spiritual aspiration dies, being no more needed; the Will of the initiate is now fixed and immovable, and astral sensitivity is no longer required.

There is a curious counterpart to this experience upon a much lower level in the death of all astral emotion which takes place for the individual aspirant at the time of the second initiation. It is then a complete episode and is consciously registered. Between the second and the third initiations, the disciple has to demonstrate a continuity of nonresponse to astralism and emotionalism. The second death, to which I am here referring, has to do with the death or the disappearance of the causal body at the time of the fourth initiation; this marks the completion of the building of the antahkarana and the institution of direct, unimpeded continuity of relationship between the Monad and the personality.

The third death takes place when the initiate leaves behind him, finally and with no prospect of return, all relation with the cosmic physical plane. This death, necessarily, lies far ahead for all in the Hierarchy and is at present only possible and permissible for a few in the Council Chamber at Shamballa. It is not, however, a process through which Sanat Kumara will pass. He underwent this "transformation" many aeons ago, during the great cataclysm which inaugurated the Lemurian Age, and which was induced by His cosmic experience and the need for an inflow of energy from extra-planetary Beings.   (17-406/7)

(7)   When all the units or cells in the body of the planetary Logos have achieved, He too is set free from dense manifestation and physically dies.   (17-414)

(8)   Here lies the secret of planetary suffering and of death. Our planetary Logos (viewing the truth from the angle of the macrocosm) is, as you know, one of the "imperfect Gods" of *The Secret Doctrine,* although perfect past our human comprehension— the comprehension of a unit in one of the kingdoms which constitutes His body of manifestation. There is still no true balance between spirit and matter, though the point of balance has almost been achieved; the involutionary forces are still potent and the spiritual energies are still frustrated, though far less so than earlier in human history; the next great human race, following on our present one, will see a point of balance reached which will usher in the so-called golden age.   (17-610)

(9)   Death is to man exactly what the release of the atom appears to be; this the great scientific discovery of the release of atomic energy has demonstrated. The nucleus of the atom releases a great light and a great potency; upon the astral plane, the phenomenon of death has a somewhat similar effect and has a close parallel in the phenomena brought about by the release of atomic energy. Every death, in all the kingdoms of nature, has to some extent this effect; it shatters and destroys substantial form and thus serves a constructive purpose; this result is largely astral or psychic and serves to dissipate some of the enveloping glamour. The wholesale destruction of forms which has been going on dur-

ing the past few years of war has produced phenomenal changes upon the astral plane and has shattered an immense amount of the existing world glamour, and this is very, very good. These happenings should result in less opposition to the inflow of the new type of energy; it should facilitate the appearance of the ideas embodying the needed recognitions; the new concepts will now be seen, and their emergence into the realm of human thinking will be dependent upon the formulation of the new "lanes or channels of impression" whereby the minds of men can become sensitive to hierarchial plans and to the purposes of Shamballa.

This, however, is by the way. My proposition will serve to show you some of the relationships between death and constructive activity, and the wide usefulness of death as a process in reconstruction. It will convey to you the idea that this great Law of Death—as it governs substance in the three worlds—is a beneficent and corrective event. Without enlarging upon it, I would remind you that this Law of Death, which governs in such potency in the three worlds of human evolution, is a reflection of a cosmic purpose which governs the cosmic etheric planes of our solar system, the cosmic astral plane and the cosmic mental plane. The death-dealing energy emanates as an expression of the life principle of that greater LIFE which enfolds all the seven planetary systems which in Themselves express the Life of our solar system. When, in our thinking and in our effort to understand, we enter this realm of pure abstraction, it is time to call a halt and draw our minds back to the more practical ways of planetary living and to the laws governing the fourth kingdom in nature, the human.   (17-503/4)

(10)   It may therefore be assumed that the Art of Elimination is practised more definitely and more effectively than was the restitution of the physical vehicle. Another point must also be considered. On the inner side, men *know* that the Law of Rebirth governs the experience-process of physical plane living, and they realise then that, prior to the elimination of the kamic, kama-manasic or manasic bodies, they are only passing through an interlude between incarnations and that they consequently face two great experiences.

1. A moment (long or short, according to the attained point in evolution) wherein contact will be made with the soul or with the solar angel.
2. After that contact, a relatively violent reorientation to earth life

takes place, leading to what is called "the process of descent and calling," wherein the man:

a. Prepares for physical incarnation again.
b. Sounds his own true note into the substance of the three worlds.
c. Revitalises the permanent atoms, which form a triangle of force within the causal body.
d. Gathers together the needed substance to form his future bodies of manifestation.
e. Colours them with the qualities and characteristics he has already achieved through life-experience.
f. On the etheric plane arranges the substance of his vital body so that the seven centres take shape and can become the recipients of the inner forces.
g. Makes a deliberate choice of those who will provide him with the needed dense physical covering, and then awaits the moment of incarnation. Esoteric students would do well to remember that parents only donate the dense physical body. They contribute naught else save a body of a particular quality and nature which will provide the needed vehicle of contact with the environment demanded by the incarnating soul. They may also provide a measure of group relationship, where the soul experience is long and a true group relation has been established.

These two critical moments are consciously faced by the discarnate man and he knows what he is doing within the limits set by his point in evolution.   (17-495/6)

(11)   First of all that the Eternal Pilgram, of his own free will and accord, chose "occultly" to die and took a body or series of bodies in order to raise or elevate the lives of the form nature which he embodied; in the process of so doing, he himself "died" in the sense that, for a free soul, death and the taking of a form and the consequent immersion of the life in the form, are synonymous terms.

Secondly, that in so doing, the soul is recapitulating on a small scale what the solar Logos and the planetary Logos have likewise done, and are doing. The great Lives come under the rule of these laws of the soul during the period of manifestation, even though They are not governed or controlled by the laws of the natural world, as we call it. Their consciousness remains unidentified with the world of phenomena, though ours is identified with it until such time that we come under the rule of the higher laws. By the occult "death" of these great Lives, all lesser lives can live and are proffered opportunity.   (17-439)

(12)   ... the *rising sign* indicates the remoter possibilities, and the spiritual goal and purpose of the immediate incarnation and of the immediate succeeding incarnations. This sign concerns itself with the struggle of the spiritual man "to carry on" from the point achieved so that when the life energy is temporarily exhausted and the "death of the personality" takes place, the man finds himself "nearer the centre of his life, closer to the centre of his group and approaching the centre of divine life," as the Ageless Wisdom expresses it. This particular phrase "death of the personality" has two definite connotations:

a. It may mean the death of the physical body, which is inevitably followed by the two stages of the death of the emotional vehicle and the subsequent dissipation of the temporary and everchanging form which the quota of mental energy has assumed during incarnation.
b. The subjective and mystical "death of the personality." This is a phrase indicating the transfer of the focus for the distribution of energy from the personality (a definite centre of force) to the soul (another definite centre).   (16-17/8)

(13)   The birth month indicates the day of opportunity. The door stands open. The particular month in which a soul comes *into* incarnation is indicated to that soul by the month in which it passed *out* of incarnation in a previous life cycle. If it, for instance, died in the month governed by the sign Leo, it will return into incarnation in the same sign, picking up the thread of experience where it left it, and starting with the same type of energy and the peculiar equipment with which it passed away from earth life plus the gain of thought and conscious onlooking. The quality of the energy and the nature of the forces to be manipulated during life are indicated to the soul in this way.   (4-436)

(14)   Therefore the use of the term "immortality" infers timelessness and teaches that this timelessness exists for that which is not perishable or conditioned by time. This is a statement requiring careful consideration. Man reincarnates under no time urge. He incarnates under the demands of karmic liability, under

the pull of that which he, as a soul, has initiated, and because of a sensed need to fulfill instituted obligations; he incarnates also from a sense of responsibility and to meet requirements which an earlier breaking of the laws governing right human relations have imposed upon him. When these requirements, soul necessities, experiences and responsibilities have all been met, he enters pemanently "into the clear cold light of love and life" and no longer needs (as far as he himself is concerned) the nursery stage of soul experience on earth. He is free from karmic impositions in the three worlds, but is still under the impulse of karmic necessity which exacts from him the last possible ounce of service that he is in a position to render to those still under the Law of Karmic Liability. You have, therefore, three aspects of the Law of Karma, as it affects the principle of rebirth:

1. *The Law of Karmic Liability,* governing life in the three worlds of human evolution, and which is ended altogether at the fourth initiation.
2. *The Law of Karmic Necessity.* This governs the life of the advanced disciple and the initiate from the time of the second initiation until a certain initiation higher that the fourth; these initiations enable him to pass on to the Way of the Higher Evolution.
3. *The Law of Karmic Transformation,* a mysterious phrase governing the processes undergone upon the Higher Way. These fit the initiate to pass off the cosmic physical plane altogether, and to function upon the cosmic mental plane. It is concerned with the release of those like Sanat Kumara, and His Associates in the Council Chamber of Shamballa, from the imposition of cosmic desire which demonstrates upon our cosmic physical plane as spiritual will. This should be to you an arresting thought. It will be obvious, however, that there is little that I can say upon this subject. The knowledge involved is not yet mine.   (17-404/5)

(15)   It might be stated, in order to sum up my general proposition, that the fear and horror of death is founded upon the love of form—our own form, the forms of those we love and the form of our familiar surroundings and environment. Yet this type of love runs counter to all our teaching anent the spiritual realities. The hope of the future, and the hope of our release from this ill-founded fear, lie in the shifting of our emphasis to the fact of the eternal soul and to the necessity for that soul to live spiritually,

constructively and divinely within the material vehicles. Into this concept again enters the thought of restitution. Wrong concepts are therefore forgotten; the idea of elimination also enters in so that right focus is attained. Integration demands consideration, so that absorption in the life of the soul will take the place of absorption in the life of the body. Sorrow, loneliness, unhappiness, decay, loss—all these are ideas which must disappear as the common reaction to the fact of death also vanishes. As men learn to live consciously as souls, as they also learn to focus themselves on soul levels and begin to regard the form or forms as simply modes of expression, all the old sorrowful ideas anent death will gradually disappear, and a new and more joyful approach to that great experience will take their place.   (17-394)

PART XIV

Resurrection is the keynote of nature; death is not. Death is only the ante-chamber of resurrection. *(13-469)*

(1) RESURRECTION is the clue to the world of meaning, and is the fundamental theme of all the world religions—past, present and the future. Resurrection of the spirit in man, in all forms, in all kingdoms, is the objective of the entire evolutionary process and this involves liberation from materialism and selfishness. In that resurrecton, evolution and death are only preparatory and familiar stages. The note and message sounded by the Christ when last on Earth was resurrection, but so morbid has been mankind and so enveloped in glamour and illusion, that His death has been permitted to sidestep understanding; consequently, for centuries, the emphasis has been laid upon death, and only on Easter Day or in the cemeteries is the resurrection acclaimed. This must change. It is not helpful to a progressive understanding of the eternal verities to have this condition perpetuated. The Hierarchy is today dedicated to bringing about this change and thus altering the approach of mankind to the world of the unseen and to the spiritual realities.   (13-469/70)

(2)   The whole concept of resurrection is the new and most important revelation which is coming to humanity, and which will lay the basis for the new world religion.

In the immediate past, the keynote of the Christian religion has been death, symbolised for us in the death of the Christ, and much distorted for us by St. Paul in his effort to blend the new religion which Christ gave us with the old blood religion of the Jews. In the coming cycle, this distorted teaching on death will assume its rightful place and be known as the disciplining urge to relinquishment and to the ending by death of the hold by matter over the soul; the great goal of all religious teaching will be the resurrection of the spirit in man, and eventually in all forms of life, from the lowest point in evolution to the highest monadic experience. The emphasis in the future will be upon the "livingness of the Christ nature"—the proof of which will be the Risen Christ—and upon the use of the will invoking this "living display."   (18-318)

(3)   The wonder of Christ's Resurrection, as far as His Personality was concerned, consisted in the fact that, after having passed through death and risen again, He was essentially the same Person, only with added powers. May it not be the same with ourselves? May not death simply remove limitation in the physical sense, leaving us with enhanced sensibilities and a clearer sense of values?   (22-244)

(4)   The fear of death is one of the great abnormalities or distortions of divine truth for which the Lords of Cosmic Evil are responsible. When in early Atlantean times they emerged from the place where they had been confined, and forced *temporarily* the retirement of the Great White Lodge to subjective levels, their first great act of distortion was to implant in human beings fear, beginning with the fear of death. From that time on, men have laid the emphasis upon death and not life, and have been ridden by fear all their days.

One of the initial acts of the reappearing Christ and of the Hierarchy will be to erase this particular fear and to confirm in peoples' minds the idea that incarnation and the taking of a form is the true place of darkness to the divine spirit which is man; it is death to the spirit temporarily, and imprisonment. Evolution, men will be taught, is in itself an initiatory process leading from one living experience to another, culminating in the fifth Initiation of Revelation and in the seventh Initiation of Resurrection.   (18-732)

(5)   There have been many deaths within the aeonial life cycle of the initiate:

1. The familiar and constantly recurring death of the physical body, incarnation after incarnation.
2. The deaths of the astral and the mental vehicles, as the undying soul discards them life after life—only to create new ones until mastery is attained.
3. Then—as a result of the incarnating process and its evolutionary effects—there comes the death of desire and its replacing by a growing spiritual aspiration.
4. Then, through right use of the mind, comes the "death" of the personality or, rather, its repudiation and renouncing of all that is material.
5. This is followed by the death or destruction of the causal or soul body at the great Initiation of Renunciation. This process of death and resurrection goes on ceaselessly in all the king-

doms of nature; each death prepares the way for a greater loveliness and livingness, and each death (if you analyse it with care) prefaces resurrection in some form or another until we come to this final resurrection and into the position of final attainment.

I will not here elaborate upon this process of constant death followed by constant resurrection, but it is the evolutionary key-note and the evolutionary technique, and only because men love unduly that which is material and hate to lose contact with the form aspect of nature do they fear death. It is wise to remember that immortality is an aspect of the living spiritual being, and is not an end in itself, as men seek to make it. To the Knowers of Life such a phrase as "I am an immortal Soul" is not even true. To say "I am Life Itself and, therefore, am immortal" approaches closer to the truth, but even that sentence is (from the angle of the initiate) only a part of a larger truth.   (18-731)

(6)   Here again I would like to pause and to point out that the concepts of death, of substitution, of the vicarious at-one-ment and of sacrifice, will—in the New Age—be superseded by the concepts of resurrection or of livingness, of spiritual unity, of transference and of service, so that a new note will enter into human life, bringing hope and joy and power and freedom.   (15-437)

(7)   The life within the form mounts up then in triumph to the bosom of its "Father in Heaven," just as the life within the physical body at the moment of death seeks its source, the Ego, and this likewise in four stages:—

1. By the withdrawal from the dense physical body.
2. By the withdrawal from the etheric body.
3. By a later vacating of the astral body.
4. A final leaving of the mental body.   (1-137)

(8)   Occultly speaking, any process of elevation or of "raising up" automatically involves *death*. This death affects the atoms in the organs involved and causes the preliminary stages of ill-health, disease and disruption, because *death is nothing but a disruption and a removal of energy*. When the science of the transference of energy from a lower centre to a higher is understood, then light will be thrown upon the entire problem of dying and the true Science of Death will come into being, liberating the race from fear.   (15-549)

(9)   "Christ is risen," is their cry, and because He has risen the kingdom of God can go forward upon earth, and His message of love can be widely distributed. They know now, past all controversy, that He has overcome death, and that in the years that lie ahead they will see death vanquished. That they expected an immediate kingdom and that they looked to see the fact of immortality universally recognised is evident from their writings and their enthusiasm. That they were mistaken, nearly two thousand years of Christianity has proved. We are not yet citizens of a divine kingdom definitely manifesting upon earth, the fear of death is as strong as ever, and the fact of immortality is still but a source of speculation to millions. But it was their sense of time that was at fault, and their failure to understand the slow processes of nature. Evolution moves slowly, and it is only today that we are truly on the verge of the demonstration of God's kingdom upon earth. Because this is the end of an age, we know that before long the hold death has on the human being, and the terror which the angel of death inspires, will disappear. They will vanish because we shall regard death as only another step on the way towards light and life, and shall realise that, as the Christ life expresses itself in and through human beings, they will demonstrate to themselves, and in the world, the reality of immortality.

The key to the overcoming of death and to the processes of realising the meaning and nature of eternity and the continuity of life can with safety be revealed only when love holds sway over the human consciousness, and where the good of the whole, and not the selfish good of the individual, comes to be the supreme regard. Only through love (and service as the expression of love) can the real message of Christ be understood and men pass on towards a joyful resurrection.   (22-233)

(10)   He reared His Cross a boundary, a symbol, and an example of method, between the world of tangible values and the world of spiritual values, and called us to the death of the lower nature in order that the Spirit of God may have full sway.

He taught us that death must end, and that the destiny of humanity is the resurrection from among the dead. Immortality must take the place of mortality. For our sakes, therefore, He rose from the dead and proved that the bonds of death cannot hold any human being who can function as a Son of God.   (22-261)

(11)   "May the energy of the divine Self inspire and
              the light of the Soul direct; may we be led from
              darkness to light, from the unreal to the real,
              from death to immortality."   (5-548)

THE CONSTITUTION OF MAN

The constitution of man, as considered in the following pages, is basically threefold, as follows:—

I. *The Monad, or pure Spirit, the Father in Heaven.*

This aspect reflects the three aspects of the Godhead:

1. Will or Power .... The Father.
2. Love-Wisdom .... The Son.
3. Active Intelligence .... The Holy Spirit.

and is only contacted at the final initiations, when man is nearing the end of his journey and is perfected. The Monad reflects itself again in

II. *The Ego, Higher Self, or Individuality.*

This aspect is potentially

1. Spiritual Will..................... Atma.
2. Intuition .... Buddhi,
   Love-wisdom, the Christ principle.
3. Higher or abstract Mind ..... Higher Manas.

The Ego begins to make its power felt in advanced men, and increasingly on the Probationary Path until by the third initiation the control of the lower self by the higher is perfected, and the highest aspect begins to make its energy felt.

The Ego reflects itself in

III. *The Personality, or lower self, physical plane man.*

This aspect is also threefold:—

1. A mental body .... lower manas.
2. An emotional body .... astral body.
3. A physical body .... the dense physical
   and the etheric body.

The aim of evolution is therefore to bring man to the realisation of the Egoic aspect and to bring the lower nature under its control.

THE SEVEN PLANES OF OUR SOLAR SYSTEM

I
DIVINE
ADI OR PLANE OF THE LOGOS
FIRST COSMIC ETHERIC

WILL

II
MONADIC
ANUPADAKA
SECOND COSMIC ETHERIC

ACTIVITY — WISDOM

III
SPIRITUAL
ATMIC PLANE
THIRD COSMIC ETHERIC

SPIRITUAL WILL
ATMIC PERMANENT ATOM

INTUITION
BUDDHIC PERMANENT ATOM

IV
INTUITIONAL
BUDDHIC PLANE
FOURTH COSMIC ETHERIC

MIND
MENTAL PERMANENT ATOM

V
MENTAL
MANASIC PLANE
COSMIC GASEOUS

EGO
EGOIC OR CAUSAL BODY
MENTAL UNIT

VI
EMOTIONAL
ASTRAL PLANE
COSMIC LIQUID

ASTRAL PERMANENT ATOM

PHYSICAL PERMANENT ATOM

VII
PHYSICAL
PHYSICAL PLANE
COSMIC DENSE

FIRST ETHER
SECOND ETHER
THIRD ETHER
FOURTH ETHER
GASEOUS
LIQUID
DENSE

THE COSMIC PHYSICAL PLANE

MONAD

TRIAD

SPIRITUAL

PERSONALITY

THE CONSTITUTION OF MAN

GLOSSARY

Adept. A Master, or human being who, having traversed the path of evolution and entered upon the final stage of that path, the Path of Initiation, has taken five of the Initiations, and has therefore passed into the Fifth, or Spiritual kingdom, having but two more Initiations to take.

Adi. The First; the primeval; the atomic plane of the solar system; the highest of the seven planes.

Atlantis. The continent that was submerged in the Atlantic Ocean, according to the occult teaching and Plato. Atlantis was the home of the Fourth Root Race, whom we now call the Atlanteans.

Antahkarana. The path, or bridge, between higher and lower mind, serving as a medium of communication between the two. It is built by the aspirant himself in mental matter.

Ashram. The centre to which the Master gathers the disciples and aspirants for personal instruction.

Astral. . . . identified with Kama or desire, and so . . . used for the plane of emotional reaction.   (4-221)

Atma. The Universal Spirit; the divine Monad; the seventh Principle; so called in the septenary constitution of man.

Atomic subplane. The matter of the solar system is divided by the occultists into seven planes or states, the highest of which is the atomic plane. Similarly, each of the seven planes is divided into seven subplanes, of which the highest is called the atomic subplane. There are therefore forty-nine subplanes, and seven of these are atomic.

Aura. A subtle invisible essence or fluid which emanates from human and animal bodies, and even from things. It is a psychic effluvium, partaking of both mind and body. It is electro-vital, and also electro-mental.

Bodhisattva. Literally, he whose consciousness has become intelligence, or buddhi. Those who need but one more incarnation to become perfect buddhas. As used in these letters the Bodhisattva is the name of the office which is at present occupied by the Lord Maitreya, Who is known in the occident as the Christ. This office might be translated as that of World Teacher. The Bodhisattva is the Head of all the religions of the world, and the Master of the Masters and the Teacher of angels and of men.

Buddha. (The) The name given to Gautama. Born in India about B.C. 621, he became a full buddha in B.C. 592. The Buddha is one who is the "Enlightened", and has attained the highest degree of knowledge possible for man in this solar system.

Buddhi. The Universal Soul or Mind. It is the spiritual soul in man (the Sixth Principle) and therefore the vehicle of Atman, the Spirit, which is the Seventh Principle.

Causal Body. This body is, from the standpoint of the physical plane, no body, either subjective or objective. It is, nevertheless, the centre of the egoic consciousness, and is formed of the conjunction of buddhi and manas. It is relatively permanent and lasts throughout the long cycle of incarnations, and is only dissipated after the fourth initiation, when the need for further rebirth on the part of a human being no longer exists.

Deva (or Angel). A god. In Sanskrit a resplendent deity. A Deva is a celestial being, whether good, bad, or indifferent. Devas are divided into many groups, and are called not only angels and archangels, but lesser and greater builders.

Devachan. That state of consciousness upon the mental plane into which the soul passes when deprived of its astral body and functioning in, or limited by, its mental body. It is of a higher order than the ordinary heaven and the bliss enjoyed is more mental than we ordinarily understand by the word, yet nevertheless it is still within the lower world of form and will be transcended when non-attachment is known.   (23-30/1)

Ego. (see Soul).

Egoic Groups. On the third subplane of the fifth plane, the mental, are found the causal bodies of the individual men and women. These bodies, which are the expression of the Ego, or of the individualised self-consciousness, are gathered together into groups according to the ray or quality of the particular Ego involved.

Etheric body. (Etheric double.) The physical body of a human being is, according to occult teaching, formed of two parts, the dense physical body, and the etheric body. The dense physical body is formed of matter of the lowest three sub-planes of the physical plane. The etheric body is formed of the four highest or etheric subplanes of the physical plane.

Hierarchy. That group of spiritual beings on the inner planes of the solar system who are the intelligent forces of nature, and who control the evolutionary processes. They are them-selves divided into twelve Hierarchies. Within our plane-tary scheme, the earth scheme, there is a reflection of this Hierarchy which is called by the occultist the Occult Hier-archy. This Hierarchy is formed of chohans, adepts, and initiates working through their disciples, and, by this means, in the world.

Initiate. From the Latin root meaning the first principles of any science. One who is penetrating into the mysteries of the science of the Self and of the one self in all selves. The Path of Initiation is the final stage of the path of evolution trodden by man, and is divided into five stages, called the Five Initiations.

Karma. Physical action. Metaphysically, the law of retribution; the law of cause and effect, or ethical causation. There is the karma of merit and the karma of demerit. It is the power that controls all things, the resultant of moral action, or the moral effect of an act committed for the attainment of some-thing which gratifies a personal desire.

Lemuria. A modern term first used by some naturalists and now adopted by Theosophists to indicate a continent that, ac-cording to the Secret Doctrine of the East, preceded Atlantis. It was the home of the third root race.

Logos. The deity manifested through every nation and people. The outward expression, or the effect of the cause which is ever concealed.

Manas, or Manasic Principle. Literally, the Mind, the mental fac-ulty; that which distinguishes man from the mere animal. It is the individualising principle; that which enables man to know that he exists, feels, and knows. It is divided in some schools into two parts, higher or abstract mind, and lower or concrete mind.

Mantrams. Verses from the Vedas. In the exoteric sense a mantram (or that psychic faculty or power that conveys perception or thought) is the older portion of the Vedas, the second part of which is composed of the Brahmanas. In esoteric phraseology mantram is the word made flesh, or rendered objective through divine magic. A form of words or syllables rhythmically arranged, so that when sounded certain vibrations are generated.

Maya. Sanskrit, "Illusion." Of the principle of form or limitation. The result of manifestation. Generally used in a relative sense for phenomena or objective appearances that are created by the mind.

Mayavi Rupa. Sanskrit, "Illusive Form." It is the body of manifestation created by the adept by an act of will for use in the three worlds. It has no material connection with the physical body. It is spiritual and ethereal and passes everywhere without let or hindrance. It is built by the power of the lower mind, of the highest type of astral matter.

Monad. The One. The threefold spirit on its own plane. In occultism it often means the unified triad — Atma, Buddhi, Manas, Spiritual Will, Intuition and Higher mind, — or the immortal part of man which reincarnates in the lower kingdoms and gradually progresses through them to man and thence to the final goal.

Permanent atom. Those five atoms, with the mental unit, one on each of the five planes of human evolution (the mental unit being also on the mental plane) which the monad appropriates for purposes of manifestation. They form a stable centre and are relatively permanent. Around them the various sheaths or bodies are built. They are literally small force centres.

Planetary Logos. This term is generally applied to the seven highest spirits corresponding to the seven archangels of the Christian. They have all passed through the human stage and are now manifesting through a planet and its evolutions, in the same way that man manifests through his physical body. The highest planetary spirit working through any particular globe is, in reality, the personal God of the planet.

Prana. The Life Principle, the breath of Life. The occultist believes the following statement: "Life we look upon as the one form of existence, manifesting in what is called matter, or what, incorrectly separating them, we name Spirit, Soul, and Matter in man. Matter is the vehicle for the manifestation of Soul on this plane of existence; soul is the vehicle for the manifestation of spirit, and these three as a trinity are synthesised by Life, which pervades them all."

Ring-pass-not. This is at the circumference of the manifested solar system, and is the periphery of the influence of the sun, both esoterically and exoterically understood. The limit of the field of activity of the central life force.

Root Race. One of the seven races of man which evolve upon a planet during the great cycle of planetary existence. This cycle is called a world period. The Aryan root race, to which the Hindu, European, and modern American races belong, is the fifth, the Chinese and Japanese belonging to the fourth race.

Shamballa. The City of the Gods, which is in the West to some nations, in the East to others, in the North or South to yet others. It is the sacred island in the Gobi Desert. It is the home of mysticism and the Secret Doctrine.

Soul. Ego or Soul, the two terms which we use as synonyms, have slightly different meanings and the difference reveals two aspects of the self-same spiritual Entity: as the Ego, he is the Son of Mind in relation to his reflection, the man in physical incarnation, and is therefore individualistic; as the Soul, he is the Son of Mind in relation to other Sons of Mind on soul levels and is therefore group-conscious and universalistic. It is quite proper to use these two words as synonyms because the spiritual Entity can manifest both aspects simultaneously—individualistic and universalistic—and is both Ego and Soul, but the student should have a clear idea of what is implied in these expressions.

Triad. The Spiritual Man; the expression of the monad. It is the germinal spirit containing the potentialities of divinity. These potentialities will be unfolded during the course of evolution. This Triad forms the individualised or separated self, or Ego.

INDEX